SuperBalance

Linda R. Silverman

The content of this book is based on the author's personal story. It is not intended to replace the advice of a trained health professional or to treat or prevent any illness. It is essential to consult a health professional.

ISBN: 9798419386358

Wishing you health and happiness

Dedicated to my father,

who always told me that anything was possible.

Contents

Introduction

This is my story of suddenly being stricken with a rare autoimmune disorder, Guillain-Barre syndrome and how I found the courage to seek the root cause of my illness and reverse it by adopting Functional Medicine protocols. Functional Medicine, as defined by the Institute for Functional Medicine, is "a biology-based approach that focuses on identifying and addressing the root cause of disease. Each symptom of differential diagnosis may be one of many contributing factors of an illness. The precise manifestation of each cause depends on the individual's genes, environment, and lifestyle, and only treatments that address the root cause will have lasting benefit beyond symptom suppression." This was achieved through the discovery and practice of SuperBalance. This is the phrase I coined to describe the result of practicing the four key factors in order to achieve vibrant health.

After many years of seeking a way to regain my health, I found a community with a cutting edge approach to treating chronic illness. Being in my situation, I developed an enormous compassion for anyone who is disabled or struggling with health issues on any level. We simply do not know what it feels like to be ill or impaired until we are faced with that circumstance ourselves. My intention is to offer a message of hope. My wish is to spare everyone facing severe health issues the long and frustrating experiences I endured. My goal, in sharing my story and the knowledge acquired in the past couple of years, is to empower people and inspire them to have the confidence to seek a new path for their own healing. There is always hope to regain our health.

Acknowledgements

With deep gratitude to my wonderful family, my children, Darcie, Ben, Heather and Chris, my brothers Robert, Alan and my dear friends Sylvia, David, Didi, Oscar, Catherine, Fred, Aleyna, Evie, Grete, Hanno, Jerald and Peter who were always there for me. My profound gratitude goes to my nutritionist, Beth Mosher, to whom I owe my life as I would not have my vibrant health today without her. Also to the many doctors and health care practitioners who treated me. I am grateful to my editor, Brooke White, who guided me through the process of writing my first book and to Lexi Ashe for designing the cover. They contributed love, support, and knowledge along the way.

Having discovered the Functional Medicine community online and via James Maskell, the Founder of the Functional Forum, I was inspired by listening to the podcasts of the extraordinary doctors including, Dr. David Perlmutter, Dr. Terry Wahls, Dr. Tom O'Brien, and Dr. Rangan Chatterjee. Through these pioneering healers and others, I connected with the latest scientific medical research on autoimmunity and this process empowered me to change my diet and lifestyle to regain my health. This experience has provided me with the knowledge and confidence to create the SuperBalance platform to help others.

May you find hope in my story and take the first steps to restore your own health knowing that SuperBalance can be achieved. Health is our most precious possession!

What Is SuperBalance?

"SuperBalance" is our unique state of balance, when all of our body's systems function harmoniously and optimal health is realized. It is the result of a personalized, whole body/holistic approach in partnership with a Functional Medicine doctor or practitioner as we take responsibility for our own health. Combining this individual approach in tandem with lifestyle and diet changes is the ticket to "SuperBalance."

My journey to achieve SuperBalance was a personal and unique adventure. It was not an easy time. It took me three years to access the knowledge I needed to understand what went wrong with my body and find the community that enabled me to feel better. I learned that if we identify and remove the triggers that disrupt our immune systems, add the micronutrients that our bodies are lacking, and adopt other key lifestyle changes, we have the ability to heal and find balance again. SuperBalance is achieved when our body's individual internal needs are adjusted for optimal performance.

The challenge is to become aware of how our bodies function, and what makes them hum without the symptoms of illness. Symptoms are a warning sign that something is out of balance in our body. To achieve SuperBalance, we must slow down, listen to our bodies, and adopt a healthier rhythm in our lives. We must find something we love to do and grasp the concept that Food is Medicine.

The SuperBalance Formula

1. Nutrition
2. Sleep
3. Stress
4. Exercise

It can be daunting to face the prospect of changing the four behaviors all at once. Start with your food intake and do one baby step at a time to change how you eat. Then look at sleep, stress and exercise. All four create the magic formula to achieve SuperBalance.

Everybody has to embark on a path of trial and error to determine what works or doesn't work in all areas of our lives. It takes effort to find the "sweet spot." It requires being mindful and aware in the moment. It means being conscious of and accepting our thoughts and feelings to begin this practice. We have to be resilient to stay the course towards vibrant health.

Foreword

Nutrition is my passion. Through working with many clients over the years, I have found that when someone is ready to make dietary and lifestyle changes to improve their overall health, the impact can be profound.

Health and wellness occur when there is a balance between the different systems. The human body is constantly working to balance itself and remain healthy based on what it is exposed to and the different environmental factors which affect it. Diet, lifestyle and how we handle our stress become very influential factors in our overall health. As a functional nutritionist, I work with clients to achieve a balance between the different body systems and we work and concentrate on different aspects of health depending on what the individual client needs

I believe the body has a tremendous ability to heal itself. There is usually a reason behind an unwanted symptom or set of symptoms. When someone doesn't feel well, it is because of several contributing factors, which create an environment for a symptom to occur. Addressing health through nutrition with a functional approach looks into different health aspects such as gut, digestive transit time, balance and timing of meals, reducing inflammatory triggers in the diet, nutrient absorption and utilization, balanced blood sugar regulation, adrenal function, thyroid function, anxiety, mood, sleep, and hydration.

A healthy gut and digestive system are the very foundation of health. When people begin to have digestive issues, inflammation often increases and influences other aspects of their wellness over time. Our digestive system consists of a microbiome that is fed by our diet. The different phylums of bacteria feed on various components within our diet, help us digest food, produce vitamins, short chain fatty acids, and produce other metabolites.

Digestive health is a very important first aspect of wellness and should be given priority. It is also highly unique to the individual. Issues such as acid reflux, pain, gas, bloating, and fast or slow transit time needs to be addressed for a healthy balance of the gastrointestinal tract. A healthy and happy digestive system is integral to our ability to break down and absorb nutrition from our diet. Any factor that adds pressure to the digestive system or affects peristalsis or the movement of food through the digestive system is going to influence nutrient absorption and affect our health over time.

Removal of inflammatory factors and supporting digestion with digestive enzymes can be a very powerful first step to improving digestion. Taking probiotics and making sure there are healthy levels of beneficial bacteria flourishing in the digestive system can also improve digestion and balance the GI tract.

The way the immune system reacts to proteins in the gut is directly related to how much inflammation is present in the gut. Functional practitioners will address microbial imbalances as well as inflammation because, when balanced, the immune system in the gut can become less reactive and autoimmune reactivity will often lower.

Autoimmunity is a process where the immune system becomes hyper-reactive and attacks itself. This type of immune system situation is very unfortunate and is considered idiopathic in nature. Healing the gut and addressing inflammatory triggers in the diet often works well to reduce digestive symptoms, inflammation, and – over time – overall immune reactivity.

Since Linda's diagnosis of Guillain-Barré syndrome, she has had quite a journey through a combined conventional and functional approach. It is my feeling that without her early diagnosis and very timely conventional treatments, she would not have had such a miraculous overall recovery and been able to quiet the over reactivity of her immune system. Her earlier treatment and steadfast mental outlook that she was going to get well and find an approach that met her needs enabled her to find the balance that she needed to regain her health.

After working to balance Linda's diet over the course of several months, her overall health improved and she no longer felt exhausted all the time. We concentrated on reducing inflammatory foods, hydrating, working on stress levels, supporting adrenal function, and promoting gut health. With adjustments to these areas, she slept better and was able to travel again and maintain her busy schedule.

Linda's mood and endurance increased as her inflammation decreased. She started absorbing her nutrition and healing her body. So, in the process of lowering stressors in Linda's diet and lifestyle as well as changing her supplements slightly, her body functioned better and was able to heal. This is exactly what the functional approach entails. It's a process that should be preventative as well as restorative.

I strongly believe that health and wellness depend on finding the (Super) Balance between the different body systems. This is influenced partly by our genetics but mostly by environmental factors, which include diet, lifestyle, and how we handle our stress. There is no greater blessing in life than health and wellness; it is precious, it should be nurtured, and it should never be taken for granted!

--Elizabeth Mosher, MS, CNS

Chapter One

Summer 2013

June

Tingling

June 1, 2013 was a rainy day. I was having breakfast with my dear friends, Didi and Oscar, whom I've known for decades. We were at the Peabody Hotel in Memphis, TN where seventy friends had gathered for the weekend to celebrate our friend Carolyn's birthday.

As an art advisor and collector based in New York, my schedule required traveling to Europe for a couple of weeks in June. I always attended the VIP opening of the Basel Art Fair and then often went to Zurich, Paris and ultimately, London to attend the contemporary auctions and bid on behalf of my clients. In 2013, this routine changed and I opted to celebrate Carolyn with the rest of our friends and miss the Venice Biennale opening in late May. I had rescheduled my plans to go to the Basel Art Fair in mid June and then travel to Venice.

At breakfast with Didi and Oscar, all of a sudden, my hands started to feel tingly. I thought the sensation was probably due to the damp weather or the air-conditioning in the hotel.

Assuming it would go away, I simply ignored it. On Sunday evening, back in New York, I kept my dinner date with my friends, Princess Jeet and her husband Nand, at our neighborhood restaurant, Cipriani, on Fifth Avenue.

When I woke up on Monday morning, I still didn't feel right and decided to skip my usual walk in Central Park. For over ten years, I'd met my friends Didi, Carolyn, and Lyanne, who had recently joined our walking group, in the park at 8 am for an hour to walk, talk and enjoy nature's glory together. We easily covered two to three miles while we caught up. I didn't know it at the time, but Friday, May 31st was the last time I would be well enough to meet my friends in the park that year.

As I tried to figure out what was wrong, I recalled a sudden spasm in my left leg the week before. It happened during a massage at home with Petri, my long-time masseur. Perhaps the spasm triggered the weirdness I was experiencing in my body? I telephoned my internist at the Center for Health and Healing, an integrative medical practice in the city. After describing my symptoms, she recommended I see a chiropractor.

The following day, Oscar helped me get an appointment with his chiropractor in order to find out if the previous week's massage had something to do with the tingling in my hands, which now had spread to my feet. The chiropractor examined me for an hour and pronounced there was nothing structurally wrong with my body. He recommended an appointment with a neurologist, which didn't seem to make any sense.

Instead, I immediately went to see my internist for an in-person consultation. She ordered blood tests and prescribed cervical, thoracic, lumbar spine, and brain MRIs. My assistant, Kris, went back and forth with my insurance company. It took countless hours and days on the phone to finally get approval for all of the tests without a diagnosis. (It's frightening to imagine how a truly sick person would be able to organize all of the tests and doctor appointments in this system on their own, especially while not feeling well.) After the original resistance and denials from the insurance company, I was finally cleared to do the MRIs. The rest of the week was devoted to getting them scheduled and done.

During this first trying week, I was on the phone with my friend, Sylvia, daily. She checked in to see how I was doing, made suggestions, and encouraged me. We've been close friends ever since we met at a wedding in Lausanne in 1978. When something was found on the cervical spine (C1, C2), Sylvia arranged for me to see a neurosurgeon at Memorial Sloan Kettering Cancer Center the following Tuesday.

I was frightened there was a tumor on my spine pressing on the nerves that would require surgery. There was a new tingling in my feet and up my legs, and I was experiencing pain in my neck, shoulders, and lower back. It was extremely difficult to sleep at night because I had to urinate every hour. I knew there was something terribly wrong. My body was weakening and losing control at a rapid pace. I needed to know what was wrong and was ready to undergo whatever it took to relieve the horrendous pain.

On June 12th, Sylvia and I met at the neurosurgeon's office for my first appointment. After his colleague performed a thorough exam, there was good news. He said the findings on the MRI had probably been there for 20 years or more and were unlikely to cause any future harm. I realized it might have been the result of a hit and run car accident I'd been in around that time. He recommended that I see a neuromuscular neurologist at New York-Presbyterian/Weill

Cornell Medical Center and arranged for an appointment the next day.

By that time, it had become difficult to walk and I was afraid of falling. I used an umbrella as a crutch to get around, and needed it on the day of my first appointment with the neurologist. After asking many questions and a thorough examination of my arms, legs, eyes, and reflexes, the neurologist pronounced a diagnosis of Guillain-Barré syndrome (GBS). I had no idea what that meant. I was just relieved and happy to have a diagnosis. I thanked the doctor and got ready to head back home.

The neurologist said he planned to admit me immediately to the emergency room. He had already contacted another neurologist to meet me there to perform a lumbar spinal tap and confirm his diagnosis. I was in a state of shock and couldn't believe what was happening. Immediately, I called my children, Darcie and Ben, and Chris, my son-in-law, to tell them what was going on. The next call was to Sylvia. Many months later, her daughter Rachel, told me, "Mommy was crying when she told me what you have." She may have known what was in store for me, but I did not.

I was assigned a space in the emergency room and waited for the second neurologist to arrive as arranged. When he got there, he pulled a curtain around my area for privacy and told me to curl up in a fetal position. He warned me that the lumbar puncture might hurt and asked if I would like to have morphine. Instead, I suggested that he announce when the thick needle was going into my spine, and I would take a deep breath to offset the pain. It was over fairly quickly. The doctor said it was the best spinal tap he'd ever done. I didn't have any reaction to it, such as a headache or pain where the needle had been inserted. My new position as an ER patient was off to a good start.

The spinal tap confirmed the GBS diagnosis but I still didn't know what it meant. The nurse arrived, took some more blood, and told me she would administer the medicine. I asked what had been prescribed and she told me it was IVIG (immunoglobulin).

The treatment was not explained to me before it was administered. Only much later did I have the time and curiosity to research it and learned that the effects last a few weeks. According to Wikipedia: "Immunoglobulin therapy is the use of a mixture of antibodies to treat a number of health conditions including HIV/AIDS, GBS and CIDP, among others. It contains antibodies against a large number of viruses."

The IVIG was in my veins for many hours throughout the night. The nurse came to check my temperature and blood pressure every fifteen minutes. The ER was very active all night. It was very noisy, all of the lights were blaring, and I got very little sleep. However, when I got up to go to the bathroom in the morning, I felt much better. The pain had gone away.

My neurologist, his team, and a group of medical students arrived by 8 am. The doctor was very pleased with the results and said I should be back to normal after four more IVIG treatments. Finally, it was explained to me that GBS is a disorder in which the body's immune system attacks part of the peripheral nervous system.

According to Wikipedia, "The peripheral nervous system (PNS) is one of the two main parts of the nervous system. The other part is the central nervous system (CNS). The PNS is divided into the somatic nervous system and the autonomic nervous system. The somatic nervous system is under voluntary control, and transmits signals from the brain to end organs such as muscles. The sensory nervous system is part of the somatic nervous system and transmits signals from senses such as taste and touch. The autonomic nervous system is a 'self-regulating' system which influences the function of organs outside of voluntary control, such as the heart rate, or the functions of the digestive systems."

Wikipedia further explained that GBS is a rapid-onset muscle weakness caused by the immune system damaging the peripheral nervous system. "The cause is unknown and the underlying mechanism involves an autoimmune disorder in which the body's immune system mistakenly attacks the peripheral nerves and damages their myelin insulation. One in 100,000 people are afflicted."

The neurologist connected the onset of GBS with a food poisoning incident I experienced after dinner in a downtown restaurant following the Jean Michel Basquiat opening the previous February. He was confident in his diagnosis and treatment plan and I was too.

After my overnight stay in the emergency room and first IVIG treatment, I was transferred to a room on the sixth floor of the neurology department. Over the course of the next four days, I had four more IVIG treatments.

Darcie brought my iPad from home and I was finally able to read about GBS. I felt incredibly lucky to have been diagnosed and treated promptly. My research informed me that the symptoms I experienced could have led to entire body paralysis. Instead, it had been a mere twelve days between the onset of the tingling in my hands and the diagnosis and first treatment. Luck was indeed on my side.

After five IVIG treatments, I felt considerably better. I regained the ability to walk on my heels and toes, which pleased the doctor. My neurologist told me, "Walk, walk, walk. Eat a balanced diet and continue with your regular schedule." And with that, I was free to leave. I was discharged and walked out of the hospital unassisted. Darcie was there to meet me, and I was thrilled to be out in the sunshine and on my way home.

Even though I had not regained my original strength, physical therapy was not prescribed. I still had mild tingling in my hands and feet but luckily there was no pain—just a sticky, tight constricted feeling in my feet. I was told that if my nerves did not regenerate within the first year, they likely never would. Although I felt much improved after being released, I never truly felt "normal" again.

Because I had planned to be away from June 10th until the end of the month, no one other than Sylvia and my immediate family knew that I had been ill or hospitalized. Having cancelled my trip to Europe, I found myself, post-hospital stay, in New York in the early summer for the first time in many years. I was free to celebrate Father's Day with Chris, Darcie, my granddaughters, Serena, who was five, and Alessandra who was two and half, and my son, Ben, who lived in Tribeca. Darcie, Chris and the girls lived in my building on the 7th floor. It's very easy to visit each other and we enjoyed a celebratory dinner together. It was a relief to have the health ordeal behind me and be at home with my family.

However, going outside to walk was a challenge. I continued to feel weak and exhausted. Doing anything at all required so much effort and energy, neither of which I could give. I could hardly walk more than a few blocks and very slowly. My new normal was to lie on my bed for many hours a day. I stayed inside and streamed Netflix for most of the first weekend after the IVIG treatments.

Ten days after I was released, I had a follow-up visit with the neurologist from New York-Presbyterian/Weill Cornell Medical Center. He performed the usual strength tests and had me get up from a chair without holding onto anything for support. The results showed improvement since the IVIG treatments. The doctor was pleased with my progress.

My question to the doctor was, "What might have caused the GBS in the first place?" It was not, as he had speculated, the food poisoning I experienced in February, having done enough research at that point to know a problem would have manifested within two weeks of the incident, instead of a full four months later. I told him that I had always had a sensitive stomach but never paid much attention to it and simply lived with it and did my best to eat mild foods. The doctor brushed this information off and suggested that my current issues could be related to the IVIG or it could be IBS. He also said I should "eat in more 5-star restaurants" to avoid future problems.

He declared I was fine so we didn't schedule another follow-up appointment. I remember thinking, "Great. If the doctor says I'm fine, I should be fine." The problem was, I was not fine. I still felt weak. I was exhausted. I found it almost impossible to do my daily yoga stretches on the floor each morning. In fact, it was difficult to get down on the floor, let alone get up. My flexibility was fading fast and in its place was a tight feeling in my hamstrings. I mentioned this to the doctor during our appointment, but he said it was nothing to worry about. Much later, I learned these sensations were due to the inflammation in my body. Inflammation was never discussed in relation to the GBS diagnosis.

July

Living with GBS

On the July 4th weekend, I drove out to Southampton with Darcie, Chris and the girls to stay with my friends, the Adlers. I enjoyed the lovely weather and the other guests while trying to convince myself that I was "fine." After all, that's what the doctor told me, even though walking up and down the staircase was difficult.

The following weekend staying with the Vidals, I was no longer able to get up at 7 am and walk around the lake in the morning, as I had enjoyed so many summers in the past. Instead, I slept until 9 am and went down for breakfast even later.

"You were once a superwoman with incredible energy, but now you're just a normal person like the rest of us," Lorraine said. I knew she was poking a little fun, but I missed my superwoman energy and wanted it back.

On Saturday evening, we attended the opening of Josephine Meckseper's sculpture exhibition at the newly opened Parish

Museum in Watermill, Long Island and then headed out to a dinner in East Hampton. The next day, we swam in the lake, but not for long as my body felt very weird. It was just a few weeks after the GBS diagnosis and the IVIG treatments and already, so much of the strength in my arms and legs was gone. I reminded myself that I needed to get back into a regular weight routine to strengthen my muscles. Little did I know, it would be my last weekend in the Hamptons in 2013.

On Sunday night, Didi and Oscar invited me for dinner on the terrace of their New York apartment. It was a humid July night and my hands and feet felt uncomfortable. That evening, after dinner, my stomach was very upset. I called the neurologist the next morning and told him what was going on. He said if it was a re-infection, I would get worse in the coming weeks.

I became very concerned about my digestion and what to eat. I was not feeling well at all and reluctantly had to cancel participating in the "Concerts in the Park" series later that week, which Didi and Oscar were sponsoring. It would have required a long walk in and out of the park before and after the concert. I was so sad to miss what was always a fun and magical evening in the city.

By the end of the week, I was miserable and significantly weaker. I broke down and called to make an appointment with the neurologist, which was set up for July 22nd. I managed to get to his office, where he accompanied me to a staircase and told me to climb up. Holding on to the railing and visibly struggling, I managed to get up the stairs. Again, he said I was "fine." He thought perhaps I was trying to do too much (although he never told me to restrict my schedule). He said the symptoms were all in my head, but if I wanted more IVIG, he would put me back in the hospital.

"YOU are the doctor. I am the patient," I responded, disturbed at our conversation. "If you tell me I'm fine, I believe you."

I began to realize I would have to deal with my stomach and the infected aspect of GBS on my own. A friend recommended that I check out a professor of clinical nursing at NYU. She was one of the country's leading clinical scientists in the area of symptom management and had been awarded 2.5 million dollars to research acupuncture and IBS. (I later learned that I had been misinformed. Her grant was to address nausea in HIV/AIDs patients, not IBS or neuropathy.) I made an appointment to see the professor, who suggested a high carb/low fat diet. She performed acupuncture on me to address my digestion and neuropathy. I felt very relaxed, but weaker when I left her office.

After a few more appointments, she recommended a woman in Huntington, Long Island who practiced Chinese herbal medicine and Amma therapeutic massage, which I had never heard of. She claimed that this woman had the ability to cure me. Marcello drove me out to Long Island the following Saturday. There was quite a lot of traffic on the way. When we finally arrived, Marcello helped me walk to the front door when he saw me struggle just to get out of the car.

The herbalist and I talked about my treatments so far, and she explained her approach. As a practitioner of Chinese medicine, she looked at the body as a "whole"—not just at the symptoms and the disease. Her opinion was that I was malnourished, which didn't make any sense. I ate well, avoided junk food and sugar, drank very little alcohol, and took lots of vitamins. How could I be malnourished?

She gave me a very light massage and prescribed several vitamins, powders, and drops for me to buy and explained what each would each do. Unfortunately, none of her supplements agreed with me. After one more session, I didn't go back. Chinese medicine did not seem to work for me. In retrospect, had I started with one product at a time, her suggestions may have proved beneficial. Trying them all at the same time was not the right approach, especially on my already compromised digestion. However, one of the books she recommended was Paul Pitchford's Healing with Whole Foods: Asian Traditions and Modern Nutrition, which pinpointed the neuropathy issue.

According to Chinese medicine, the spleen governs the transportation and transformation of water and food throughout the body. If the spleen is cold, or nonfunctioning, it is almost impossible to change. This was the first insight into how my body was not working. Several months later, my thoughts returned to the herbalist's diagnosis of malnourishment and it resonated with me. Could malnourishment be the cause of the GBS?

I celebrated my 65th birthday on July 23rd with zero energy and exhausted all the time. I remember thinking, "Now, I know how it feels to be old." Until June, I felt immune to the aging process. My body was able to do what my mind planned. I traveled constantly and exercised daily. Longing for those days, I simply refused to accept that this new debilitated self was how my life would be.

I didn't feel well enough to celebrate my birthday that evening in a restaurant. Instead, we had a lovely dinner at Darcie and Chris's apartment with Ben, Serena, and Alessandra. Looking back at the birthday pictures from that night, I can see the fear and weakness in my face and how much thinner I'd become.

During the summer of 2013, I avoided most of the invitations I received and invented a lot of excuses, saying it was too hot to go out or suggesting getting together the following week. When the next week arrived, I made another excuse as I did not want to reveal to anyone what was going on, mainly because I didn't know or understand what was going on myself. I worried that by telling my friends and colleagues about the GBS diagnosis, they would Google it and feel sorry for me. The last thing I needed was pity, and absolutely did not want to hear any negative comments or have negative energy around me.

Upon waking every day, I sat in my library and read affirmations about infections leaving my body. I thought about my stomach improving, and imagined what it would be like to be well and strong again. I read and cried a lot but I also knew that one day, the affirmations would be true. I will be fine! It gave me courage to align my thoughts with words. My goal was to turn defeat into victory and illness into health.

"Mind over matter" is not a medical strategy, but it was a practice that resonated with me and gave me hope. I never accepted the illness label, even after five IVIG treatments. I always visualized myself as a strong and healthy person. It never would have occurred to me to give up. I was determined to keep on going from Plan B to C all the way to Z if necessary. The fighting spirit has always been within me.

Whenever Serena and Alessandra were playing games in my apartment, or working on art projects, and encountered a difficult problem, I suggested they try Plan B. "What's Plan B?" they asked. I told them about Winston Churchill's "Never give up speech" that he gave at his old school, Harrow: "Never give up. Never give up. Never, never, never-never-never!"

One afternoon, Alessandra was complaining about not being able to do something and I overheard Serena tell her, "Alessandra, if it's not working out, go to plan B and then C and all the way to Z. Never give up, just like Winston Church said." I was so happy when I heard the older sister reminding her younger sister of this critical life lesson. Alessandra got it. She found a solution to her problem and was happy again.

Imagine how much better off we would all feel if we could simply adopt this mantra? We all need to learn not to panic when things get tough and don't go our way. Complaining doesn't move the needle forward. The best course of action is to move on from the problem and redirect our attention to finding possible solutions. How we think is how our lives unfold. Think well; be well!

A few days after the girls were over, I went on a brief business trip to New Canaan to visit one of my clients. Marcello had to help me out of the car again and carry the art books into the house. I struggled to act like everything was fine (as indeed, the doctor said it was) but there was no denying that my body was quickly becoming weaker again. My lack of energy was a deep concern, despite my positive mental outlook.

On July 31st, I had to call the neurologist once again. He told me to go to the ER and said he would meet me there. My assistant, Kara, insisted on going to the emergency room and staying with me. She started working for me in late June and had only ever seen me in this weakened condition.

It took all afternoon for the neurology team to assess and reassess me. One of the female neurologists asked me to squeeze her hands, which is a standard strength test. She said my grip was good. I told her, "With all due respect, I think you have very weak hands! I am no longer able to walk on my heels and I feel weak and exhausted all the time." Regardless, because I had a strong handgrip and was able to walk ten feet without falling down, they were reluctant to admit me. Eventually, they relented.

While waiting for my room to be available, I asked the nurse if there was a quiet place to use the phone so I could call one of my clients. There was no cell service in the ER. The nurse brought me to an office with police officers stationed outside of it. Amidst the chaos and shrieking sirens of the ER, I was able to place an important Franz Kline painting in a major collection.

While all of this was going on, Didi tried to reach me at my office. When she couldn't get anyone on the phone, she called my cell and asked what was going on. I told her I was in the ER at New York/Presbyterian Hospital/Weill Cornell Medical Center. She immediately came and relieved Kara, who had stayed long past when it was time for her to go home.

After six hours of sitting on a gurney in the middle of the emergency room activities, it was time to be admitted. No wonder they thought I was fine. In comparison to everyone else in the ER, I was in pretty good shape. I was able to walk and squeeze hands and certainly wasn't causing any disturbance.

When I got to my room on the sixth floor, I finally told Didi about my GBS diagnosis. She was shocked and upset that I hadn't told her sooner. I explained to her that she was out of town when the first episode occurred. I told her that Sylvia had been totally involved and helpful every step of the way and was constantly checking up on me.

It was an uncomfortable conversation because Didi is one of my dearest friends. I tried to explain that having an acute onset of a dreaded illness, which I did not fully understand or accept, was too foreign for even me to get my head around. I was simply unable to share my illness with anyone but my family and had intentionally kept it private. As a single woman who ran my own art advisory business, I didn't think it necessary for all of New York (or even my close friends) to know I was sick. I envisioned myself as a healthy person and believed this thing would resolve itself and I'd be back to normal in no time. No such luck. Didi wrote down my diagnosis and said she would research it and find out what it meant and come back to visit the next day.

I did not have the same immediate results from the IVIG treatment as the previous month. My neurologist said sometimes it takes longer to have an effect.. He described my condition as a GBS flare up, which is apparently very unusual. After four more IVIG treatments, I was released on August 3, 2013 with a prescription for physical therapy.

Ben came to meet me and take me home. I rested that afternoon from the ordeal, but the next day, I had a crashing headache from the IVIG. In a follow-up conversation with the hospital, I was told that it was perfectly normal to have a headache after the treatment and advised to take Tylenol and drink lots of water.

August

My Body is Collapsing

The following week was my first appointment with the physical therapist for an evaluation and a short session, which I had requested the neurologist prescribe to improve my strength. At that point, I needed a cane to walk although I used it reluctantly. Despite the fact that the physical therapy office was only a few blocks from my apartment, on 57th and 7th, I took a taxi both ways. After my visit, I was encouraged that the therapy would help me to get stronger. I was given a sheet of exercises to do at home, which I struggled to do each day.

After a few weeks of physical therapy, my body went limp on the mat. We stopped the exercises and the therapist took me to a room to lie down. When I got home later that day, all I felt like doing was resting. The only way to describe the feeling was a stickiness or tightness. My limbs were weak and listless. It felt like they lacked adequate circulation. My body did not feel like my own. The current one was weird and unstable. So much for building up my strength. It was the last physical therapy appointment I had.

On August 27th, I returned to New York-Presbyterian/Weill Cornell Hospital Medical Center for a third round of IVIG. This time, the neurologist's office organized my room on the sixth floor in advance, and there was no delay. After a few days of treatments, I got a little boost of energy and was discharged on the 29th. Upon returning home, I felt so incredibly weak and was very concerned about not recovering properly, not being given any guidance on how to live with the disease or how to get better.

Chris recommended seeking another opinion and I agreed to his suggestion. My online research led me to the GBS/CIDP Foundation website, where I discovered a neurology professor at Johns Hopkins Hospital. His focus was on neuromuscular diseases with a special emphasis on peripheral neuropathies. He was considered an expert in GBS and CIDP and was affiliated with the international arm of the foundation. There was no such doctor in New York.

I reached out to the neurologist via email and he responded the same day. He requested to see my hospital records before we made an appointment to meet in Baltimore. During our correspondence, he asked if I had received the CIDP (chronic inflammatory demyelinating polyneuropathy) diagnosis. My neurologist had never mentioned this condition. When researching it online later, I discovered that CIDP is the chronic form of GBS. It occurs in 1 out of 3.5 million people and is a disorder of the peripheral nervous system (PNS). The PNS includes all of the nerves in the body that lie outside the spinal cord and the brain. These nerves carry information to and from the central nervous system to provide complex body functions.

I was desperate to understand what was going on in my body and what the diagnosis of autoimmune disease meant for me. Further research online led me to a book by Dr. Imran Khan called The Flame Within. Dr. Khan is an Indian neurologist and his book focuses on the prevention, diagnosis, and potential treatment of autoimmune disorders. He covered remedies I was unfamiliar with at the time: herbal, homeopathic, chelation, allopathic, holistic electronic, oxygenation, and natural cures.

A chapter in Dr. Kahn's book about CIDP resonated with me on two key points. He said that excessive exercise and the lack of essential fatty acids in the body were possible causes of the condition. He suggested a change of diet to compensate for the lack of certain vitamins and minerals. His words reminded me of the Amma therapist in Long Island and her suggestion that my body was malnourished. Perhaps, she had a point after all.

I had always questioned why the doctors never looked at the inflammatory markers in my blood, which were very high. They simply accepted it as part of the problem without digging deeper. Specifically, CRP (or C-reactive protein) is a blood test marker for inflammation in the body. It is produced in the liver and its level is measured by testing the blood.

My questions were always related to what the cause of my problem was. I was consistently told, "we don't know." I never understood that answer because it didn't make any sense. They said, "Even though it's chronic, don't worry. It won't kill you." That response didn't sit quite right either. I wasn't prepared to just take pharmaceuticals forever. There was no way I was going to live my life in and out of the hospital, feeling weaker and weaker with each treatment, or degenerating into a wheelchair.

I totally believed something in my body had gone wrong, and if my body got what it needed, it would heal over time. I never wavered from that belief no matter how weak my body became. My mother lived to 93 and my father to 85 without major illnesses, so I was convinced that remaining active well into my 80s was a sure thing. Being struck down in my 60s made no sense to me at all and I refused to accept it. Denial was a powerful motivator on the road to healing and it was my goal to beat this weird sudden health issue.

The more I researched and read about the peripheral nervous system and the myelin sheath, the more hope I had to be well. Myelin is an insulating layer that forms around nerves, including those in the brain and spinal cord. It's made up of protein and fatty substances. Its function is to facilitate the conduction of electrical impulses through the nerve cells.

Despite my frustration with my situation, I had been very fortunate in many ways. I was diagnosed and treated early – just twelve days after my first symptoms – and I never lost feeling in my hands and feet. I had not experienced permanent nerve damage. Armed with my new information and the realization that my nerve damage was relatively mild, it seemed there was an excellent chance for the nerves to regenerate. I imagined that all I needed was a reboot to my system, not unlike recharging a cell phone or a laptop.

In the meantime, however, uncertainty lingered. Each morning, before I got out of bed, I wondered if my condition had worsened in the night and if I would be able to walk. I anticipated when I would have to sit down or lie down to rest and wait for my assistant to come to the apartment at 10 am before stepping into the shower. I was concerned about falling and not being able to get up by myself. This level of dependency had never happened and I didn't like it. Something had to give.

Chapter Two
Autumn 2013

September

Second Opinion, Second Diagnosis

After making excuses that I wasn't free for dinner for weeks, I finally admitted to my friend, Jerald, that I hadn't been going out at all recently with anyone.

"Okay, Blondie," he said, undeterred, "How about this: I'll come to you and bring dinner from Quality Meats. We'll watch the US Open together. Say, next Saturday?"

His suggestion was easy and I was delighted. Since he was my guest, I ordered the steaks and asked him to pick them up. Even though Quality Meats is five steps out of the back entrance of my apartment building, I wasn't able to carry anything or navigate the few steps to enter the restaurant. Jerald graciously agreed and arrived on Saturday with the steaks and a bottle of red wine. It was fairly easy to organize the dinner. We brought the food into the library to watch the tennis matches as we ate. We had a lovely evening and I was delighted to see Jerald again after being cooped up for so many weeks.

On September 18th, I had my first appointment with the neurologist at John Hopkins in Baltimore. Didi picked me up and we took the train down together. She was my emotional support as well as my physical cane. Without her assistance, I could not have made the trip.

During our initial meeting, my new neurologist asked why I had come to see him. I told him to find the root cause of my illness. He asked a lot of detailed questions and we spent over an hour discussing my recent medical history. He performed the standard neurological physical exam to test my eyes, arms, legs, feet, reflexes, and flexibility and had me walk on my toes and heels. He ordered an EMG (electromyography) test, which is an electrical test of the nerves and muscles on my legs. It was quick and painless, unlike the test the New York neurologist performed in June.

After a thorough appointment, examination, and round of testing, the new neurologist announced, as he suspected, I had CIPD. He said he would recommend a lower dose of IVIG to my neurologist in New York, and that if I were his patient in Baltimore, he would arrange to have treatment administered at home. What a novel idea! I felt reassured in his expert hands. He gave me a list of all sorts of X-rays and blood tests to be performed back home at New York-Presbyterian Hospital/Weill Cornell Medical Center. I was very impressed with him, as was Didi, and we returned to New York the same day.

A few days after the trip to Johns Hopkins, my body weakened again to the degree that I had to go back to the hospital. Didi was kind enough to take me over there. My neurologist was not on call that day and the covering physician was unable to lower the IVIG dose, so he simply administered the old, higher dose. He also ran some blood work.

I was extremely frustrated. How could I end this cycle of hospitalization and IVIG treatments? The pattern seemed to be a mild pick up, followed by debilitating headaches, and an eventual decline. The routine was intolerable.

I was sad to miss Serena's fifth birthday with her friends at The Party Place and asked Darcie not to mention that I was in the hospital, as I didn't want my granddaughter to worry or see me as a patient. A few days later, I was discharged from the hospital once again.

The day I was released, one of my colleagues, Graham, was in town from London and wanted to meet downtown for lunch. It was too difficult for me to leave the neighborhood and suggested The Ritz Carlton Hotel, next door to my apartment building. We met at the bar. I had a little trouble climbing onto the bar stool, but otherwise was fine and didn't mention that I had literally just been discharged from the hospital. In my mind, when it's over, it's over. I was out. It was time to move on. I didn't need to talk about it.

The following week, the tests that the Johns Hopkins neurologist had prescribed were done. Despite his recommendations, they did not reveal the structural cause of my illness. I was scheduled for another IVIG treatment in a few days. While in the hospital undergoing these tests, I began to feel extremely weak and called the neurologist's office. It had only been two weeks since my previous treatment and now I was struggling to walk two steps and felt awful. His office was able to arrange for a room the next day.

This time, the IVIG dose was much lower – at the recommendation of my new neurologist – but the treatment didn't seem to have any effect at all. I still was unable to walk on my heels or my toes and had no energy. What good did the IVIG do for me? Nothing! In fact, it made me even weaker.

Ben came to take me home and I left the hospital in a wheelchair. When I got back to my apartment, I went straight to bed and fell asleep. Waking up later, I was too weak to make dinner. Darcie came over to help me. Afraid I wouldn't be able to get up and walk to the bathroom in the morning, I left a couple of canes near the bedside. After this hospitalization and IVIG treatment, I felt even weaker than before and was extraordinarily worried about what was going on.

Early October

Rock Bottom & Rebound

The next morning, while sitting on the toilet seat, my legs buckled and I landed in the bathtub. How did this happen? What was going on with my body? I was in a panic, totally frightened and shocked. Although I hit the side of my head and felt a bump, I knew nothing was broken. It was 7:00 am and no one was scheduled to come to the apartment that day as Kara had the day off for the long Columbus Day weekend. I couldn't stay in the bathtub, but I couldn't call anyone for help either because there wasn't a phone nearby.

Suddenly, I summoned up all my courage and strength and said to myself, "Get out of the bathtub now!" I turned onto my side and lifted one leg over the side of the tub and then the other and crawled on my hands and knees to my bedroom and grabbed my cell phone from the side table. I emailed the New York neurologist, who responded by advising me to "get an aide" and then told me to "take care." Frustrated, I emailed the Baltimore neurologist next. He responded immediately and told me to return to the hospital at once.

In between emails to the doctors, I contacted my children. Chris ordered breakfast for me and the delivery man opened my apartment door and brought the food inside. Sylvia arranged for an aide to help me gather my things and take me to the hospital. The staff was shocked to see me back the day after I had been released. When the doctor on call heard that I fell, he immediately ordered a cat scan on my head, even though I assured him I was fine and only had a little bump in the back of my head. As I suspected, the scan came back normal.

Back in my hospital room, I was told that the next course of action was a steroid IVMP (intravenous methylprednisolone), which sent me into a panic. According to Wikipedia, "This corticosteroid is used as an inflammatory or immunosuppressant agent for diseases of hematologic, allergic, inflammatory, neoplastic and autoimmune origin." I knew from my research that this was the third treatment choice and it was not well tolerated by most patients.

IVMP has many unpleasant side effects including insomnia, anxiety, easy bruising, gastrointestinal stress, headaches, and a few other undesirable potential reactions. The second treatment choice is plasmapheresis, which is a method of removing blood from the body, separating it into plasma and cells, and transfusing the cells back into the bloodstream. It is used to treat autoimmune conditions by removing antibodies. Plasmapheresis had not been mentioned by anyone, and of course, I'd already thoroughly explored the IVIG treatment option and didn't understand why we were skipping directly to option three.

I emailed the Baltimore neurologist to express my concern about the steroid treatment and he called me immediately. As usual, he was very reassuring and encouraged me to focus on getting better instead of worrying about the potential side effects of the treatment. Without reservation, I agreed to the treatment, as I trusted him.

The IVMP steroids were administered later that evening. Within minutes, it felt like lightning was shooting through my body and I was ready to get out of the hospital bed and dance. It seemed that my former energy was coming back, stronger than ever before. That night, I got very little sleep as every sound in the hospital floor and out on the street was magnified. After two more treatments, I was buzzing as if I'd been shot full of electricity.

On Friday night, Darcie stopped by the hospital to visit and see how I was doing. She brought some food and my noise cancellation headphones. My hearing was still heightened as I heard every sound from within the hospital floor as well as the outside sounds from the traffic below. She was very concerned and didn't feel comfortable leaving.

Even though Chris and the girls were waiting for her in the car to go out to their house in Sagaponack for the long weekend, she offered to send them on their way and stay with me. Reassuring her that I was fine and had already arranged for my nurse aide, Mahonie, to bring me home when the time came, and I would be much happier if Darcie went away for the weekend as planned and texted me beautiful images of the family having fun, instead of sitting around worrying about me in the hospital. Reluctantly, she agreed and we said goodbye.

On Saturday, my friend Grete came by to visit. We became friends and colleagues at Sotheby's decades ago. I joked with her and said, "Today is a good day. I only need one cane to go to the bathroom!" which was about three steps from my bed. We laughed and it felt good to be on the mend. Whenever there's a ray of light or hope in my life, I reach out for it.

The next day, a nurse came around and handed me a pill to swallow. I asked her what it was for and she said it was an insulin pill for diabetes. Quickly, I told her that I didn't have diabetes and she replied, "But you will. Your blood sugar will continue to rise because of the steroid treatment, which is one of the things we monitor." I refused to take the insulin pill and asked her to get the doctor or mark in my file that I'd refused the pill. What were they thinking?

Before I was released, the attending female neurologist came in to have a chat with me. We talked about the treatments and my concerns about steroids. When the first three protocols for GBS (IVIG, plasmapheresis, and steroid IVMP) are exhausted, the fourth course of action is chemotherapy to suppress the immune system. The attending neurologist presented several chemotherapy drug options and told me about the success many people have with them. She also discussed the strong possibility that I could end up in a wheelchair.

I was outraged and didn't want to hear any part of what this doctor was saying. None of it resonated with me and told her that I had no intention of being an invalid for the rest of my life. Her plan had nothing to do with getting well! There had to be a better route to wellness than chemo for an autoimmune disorder. The conversation did not end on a good note and she left abruptly. No doubt, she logged an entry into my chart about what a difficult and resistant patient I was.

Shortly after this blow up with the doctor, I was discharged with many prescriptions for at home services including a six-week round of steroids, a visiting nurse, and a physical therapist. My aide took me home and we went directly to the hairdresser. I needed something to lift my spirits and afterwards, we sat in the park together. I already felt better just being out of the hospital and sitting in the warm sunshine. My aide took a picture of me smiling on a bench in Central Park. I sent it to my children with the caption: "Lili's back." Lili is the name my granddaughters call me.

The physical therapist came to my apartment a few times a week and gave me exercises to do every day to strengthen the legs. She encouraged me to climb stairs and walk around the block, even though I needed to sit down every five minutes, which we did in a nearby restaurant. It was exciting to take a step in the right direction, even though I needed someone by my side to go out. I wasn't ready to be on my own, but was definitely working toward independence.

I had been in the hospital six times in five months. The steroids definitely helped me to regain my strength. The Baltimore doctor kept in touch to follow my progress. My side effects were powerful, but from what I had read, they were not as bad as they could have been. A lot of people cannot tolerate steroids and that's easy to understand as I'd heard about various reactions including anger, depression, and weight gain. Apparently, steroids exaggerate a person's underlying characteristics and unique moods.

In my case, I was starving and ate all day long and still got up in the middle of the night to eat again. The drugs made me feel very hyper and I was talking a mile a minute. My skin became very dry. Unlike many people, I never gained weight and never got what is referred to as "moon face," which is when the cheeks swell up and cause an overall puffy look. All in all, I tolerated the steroids well. In fact, they were the turning point in my treatment and stopped my rapid decline. Thanks to my Baltimore neurologist.

At the end of October, as I slowly began to regain my strength, the thought of going to an art opening or exhibition alone was very worrisome. When I needed someone to accompany me, my friend, Peter, was often by my side for many events. He was a great sounding board for the various research discoveries I made over the upcoming months and years.

Late October

Living With CIDP

The Baltimore neurologist invited me to attend his lecture in Stony Brook University, Long Island on "Living with CIDP." It was of great concern how to make the two-hour trip by myself. Grete kindly offered to accompany me. We arranged for Marcello to drive us out to Long Island and back. At that point, I was walking much better but still needed the cane to go out. My energy had improved, but I tired easily and was constantly apprehensive about trying to figure out what I could and couldn't do and how to manage my life.

At the lecture, it was fascinating to see the neurologist's other patients and observe their various stages of mobility. Some needed help walking and used walkers or canes; many were obese and unhealthy looking; some looked absolutely fine. Surveying the audience, I felt comparatively healthy and left my cane beside the chair. (I always think I look the healthiest in a group, even when I was in the hospital.) In truth, my health was excellent: I had been exercising, lifting weights, and stretching daily for decades. Apparently, my body held up rather well under the barrage of IVIG and steroid IVMP treatments. All I needed to do was get over my weird health issue once and for all and return to my fully energetic and mobile self.

The lecture was very interesting. The doctor used graphs to illustrate patient improvement statistics as related to the various pharmaceutical protocols offered. A Q&A followed the presentation. One man stood up and said he had suffered with CIDP for over ten years. He endured debilitating pain from the neuropathy and had not been able to work for many years. He also suffered from major depression. He said he saw a woman in Connecticut who gave him medical messages and herbal teas that she claimed removed the toxins from his body. The woman's treatments helped him tremendously with the pain and increased his mobility. He sought the doctor's opinion of such an approach. The neurologist replied, "There is no scientific evidence to support such treatment," and then he moved on to the next question.

Immediately, I turned around and told the man that we should talk at the break. We exchanged information, and the following week, Steve and I began a dialogue about his situation over the last ten years and how he was improving. This mysterious woman in Connecticut was intriguing and I started to strategize how to get up to her home, two and a half hours from the city, and look into her treatments first hand.

November

High on Steroids

Weeks passed. As I was still so hyper from the steroids, which caused my head to spin around and prevented me from thinking clearly, I was unable to make the trip on my own for a follow-up visit with the Hopkins neurologist. The plan was to go one Sunday evening to meet him in New Jersey, where he was attending a medical conference the next day. Grete and I took a car service together to meet him where I announced that I wished to get off the steroids.

He was pleased with my progress and recommended weaning me off by lowering the dosage gradually. I also mentioned that my next challenge was to attend the Miami Art Fair in early December. It would be my first time traveling by airplane in six months – a big step indeed. He said that, given how much I had already improved, it would definitely be possible to make the trip. Grete suggested travelling with her and Hanno instead of traveling alone, which was greatly appreciated.

After returning home, I happily made my flight reservations to Miami. Normally, I would spend four or five nights there during the art fair, but this time I only booked two nights. The doctor had said to pace myself; two nights and three days was a big deal given what I had been through in the last six months.

Chapter Three
Winter 2013 - 2014

December

Art Basel Miami Beach

It was exciting to have my doctor's approval to travel. However, I was anxious about taking the trip as I planned to meet some of my clients at the VIP opening and worried what would happen if I couldn't keep up or needed to rest. I was skilled at the art of pretending to be fine, but being out of town with clients caused me considerable anxiety.

The flight to Miami went smoothly. We had to walk through the entire airport to get to the car rental agency, but my legs and stamina held up well. So far, so good.

The first evening, I attended the opening of the Perez Museum, which involved a lot of walking. My friend, Patrice, accompanied me and often I had to hold onto his arm for support when feeling wobbly. Afterwards, we went to the Tracey Emin opening at the Miami Contemporary Art Museum followed by dinner with friends and clients. The evening ended at the White Cube party at the Soho House.

At 11:30 p.m., I announced it was time to go back to the hotel. I had not exactly been pacing myself; quite the opposite and I had a full schedule planned for the following day. I intended to be up early for Eli Broad's talk with his architect, Elizabeth Diller. They would discuss his new museum, The Broad, scheduled to open in downtown LA the following year.

I felt fine in the morning. The lecture was held in the New World Symphony building, designed by Frank Gehry. It was a short distance from my hotel and afterwards, I walked over to the Convention Center to meet my clients. It was thrilling to be back in the action of the art world.

On Thursday morning, I checked out of the hotel and was driven to the collections I wished to see before leaving town: the Rubell family collection, Martin Margulies, and Rosa de la Cruz in the Wynnwood section. The last stop was the VIP opening of NADA back in Miami Beach before heading to the airport.

Rushing around from one art exhibit to the next made me think about all I had missed due to my illness: the June art events in Europe, the Chicago Art Fair in September, the London Frieze Art Fair, and FIAC in Paris in October. I kept thinking, "I'll be better in time to go to Chicago," or "I'll make it to London," but never felt confident or strong enough to book the trips. It was safer to stay at home in my apartment, which was organized for my comfort and peace of mind. I had managed to go to Peter Brant's opening for Julian Schnabel in Greenwich and the contemporary auctions in New York in November, but the trip to Miami marked my comeback.

After the day's activities, I caught an early afternoon flight back to New York. I was able to manage the hectic Miami airport by myself with a carry-on and made it home in time for dinner at Didi and Oscar's at 7:30 p.m. – a miracle indeed! How happy I was to be amongst my friends and their guests and enjoy a wonderful holiday evening. The trip to Miami was a giant step forward in my recovery and restored my confidence to be well again.

January

A New Direction

Steve, from the "Living with CIDP" lecture on Long Island, and I stayed in touch on the phone. He encouraged me to go to Miami and checked in when I got home to see how things went. He was pleased to hear the trip was such a success.

Under my doctor's supervision, I was weaned off the steroids by late December. Since I was "drug-free," Steve suggested getting me an appointment with the woman he had been seeing in Connecticut for medical massage and detoxing teas. He asked me a lot of questions before we settled on a date for a visit.

It took some planning, but Steve recommended I take the train from Grand Central Station to Scarsdale, where he would pick me up and drive two hours to Connecticut. He would have his massage and wait while I had mine and then we'd drive back to Scarsdale. Of course, I appreciated his kind offer and agreed to the plan, but was worried about getting on an early train and managing all of the stairs in the station on my own. The fear of my body being uncooperative or unresponsive was constant and it factored into every decision.

Boldly, I decided to go for it and finally meet the famous masseuse therapist in person. She was a warm, jovial Russian woman of a certain age and girth, and at our first meeting, I believed she would help me. Her home was located in a beautiful, quiet town and I felt better just breathing in the fresh air. At the initial consultation, we discussed my recent medical history including hospital stays, medications, and blood tests.

After our chat, it was time for my medical massage. I lay face down on the massage table naked in a very cold room. When she touched my feet, I screamed out in pain. It felt like she was using knives to separate the inside of the balls of my feet. My nerves were bundled together and damaged; they were not happy being disturbed and pounded. Trained as a pediatrician in Russia, she said the attention she paid to my feet would regenerate the nerves and prevent further degeneration. Steve warned me that the massage may be painful but it was excruciating and barely tolerable!

After slapping my feet, she moved onto my legs, lower back, shoulders, neck, and head – slapping each in turn. She also worked on my hands and forearms. After she moved away from my sensitive feet, her touch was amazing – strong and soft at the same time. I had never had a massage like hers before. When it was over, I dressed and walked into the living room where her other patients waited for their massages.

She handed me my teas in two large bottles on my way out. They were made from herbs imported from Russia. She told me to come three times a week if I wanted to see a real difference and explained that the teas would detoxify my body and heal the neuropathy. My feet and legs felt different – lighter. I moved and felt much better when I walked down the wooden stairs to the car. Wow! Steve was onto something.

During the first month, I went back to see the therapist three times weekly and then bi-weekly for the next six months. In the beginning, after returning home from the massage treatments, I went to bed immediately and slept for an hour or two, feeling totally exhausted. Little by little, my fatigue subsided and my energy slowly increased.

During my visits, I made connections with other patients who offered to meet me at various train stations in Connecticut to drive together. Throughout the coldest early winter mornings, I left my apartment in the dark at 6:30 am to catch a train, meet up with other patients, and make the drive.

I always looked forward to my excursions to Connecticut and it was a pleasure to meet and swap medical stories with other patients. We learned from each other. It was a special club for patients suffering with pain and degenerating illnesses. It was a place where we could say how we felt. We shared our concerns about our bodies and our hopes of getting our health back. I kept the subject of my illness a secret from most of the people I knew. It was easier to avoid any conversation about this complication in my life. In my journal at the time I wrote, "It is my wish to one day share my story to help as many people as I can. I want others to know there is the possibility of healing outside the conventional medical community."

February

The GBS/CIDP International Foundation

In the winter of 2014, the Baltimore neurologist introduced me to the founder of the GBS/CIDP International Foundation. He thought she and I would have a lot to talk about, and he was right. The organization's roots are embedded in a story both personal and familiar. In 1979, her husband – an active, healthy man – suffered from a very bad cold. A week later, he was completely paralyzed. He was diagnosed with GBS, at the time treatment options were extremely limited. He spent a month in the ICU taking steroids under medical supervision, at which point he and his wife decided to start a GBS support group. In 1981, it expanded into the vibrant foundation it is today.[1]

It took four months in rehab for him to learn how to walk, plus additional therapy to regain fine motor control. He couldn't walk backwards for another five years. With time and research, he eventually regained his strength enough to play tennis and ride a bicycle; activities he enjoyed before GBS. He lived for another 33 years after his diagnosis.

---

[1] https://www.gbs-cidp.org/about/history/

When I read about cases like this after my own diagnosis, I knew I was lucky that my attack was comparatively mild. Despite the fact that I had almost no energy or stamina and a difficult time walking, the damage to my peripheral nervous system was relatively limited. Nevertheless, I was passionate about learning more about the disease, its treatment, and most importantly, the root cause.

The founder and I arranged a lunch in New York with the executive director of the foundation, whose father-in-law was diagnosed with GBS. Ten years later; her son was diagnosed as well. Following her son's recovery, the executive director became the parent liaison for the foundation and was deeply involved with the organization.

It was difficult for me to walk the two blocks to meet the ladies at the restaurant on 60th and Fifth Avenue. I was still in the early stages of my treatments with the massage therapist in Connecticut and had not yet regained my full strength and stamina. At lunch, we discussed the possibility of me hosting a cocktail party at my home for the New York members, patients, and supporters of the GBS/CIDP Foundation. The party was scheduled for mid-April. Very few of my friends knew that anything was wrong with me, and the women from the Foundation wanted me to share my story at the party.

Chapter Four
Spring 2014

April

Insight Into Nutrition: *Grain Brain* by David Perlmutter

The GBS/CIDP Foundation cocktail wound up being my coming out party just as the women who planned it had hoped. Along with their list of guests, including a group that came in specifically for the party and returned to Pennsylvania the same evening, I invited several of my friends as well as Darcie, Chris, and Ben.

I shared my story and introduced my Baltimore neurologist to everyone, with much gratitude, for all of his help. He gave a brief presentation, after which one of my good friends rushed over and said, "Why didn't you tell us what was going on? We are going through this too!" She told me her brother was diagnosed with CIDP ten years prior and was very depressed and in a wheelchair. I assured her that no one knew and asked her to please understand I was simply not ready to divulge my diagnosis.

At one point during the evening, a woman approached me and said, "You must feel very lonely suffering with this illness." One of the main reasons I never talked about it was because I never wished to have conversations like that with anyone, let alone a stranger! I told her that I never felt lonely because I was surrounded by my family and close friends, and then I asked her who she was. She told me she was from the pharmaceutical company. WTF? What was this woman doing in my home? She said the neurologist had invited her.

Later that month, my friend Aleyna called me at home one evening. She and I often met at the Stamford RailRoad station and drove to see the massage therapist together. Full of excitement, she said, "I know what caused your problem. Gluten!" I replied, "How is that possible since my test for celiac was negative many years ago?" She recommended that I read Grain Brain by Dr. David Perlmutter. He is a world-renowned, board certified neurologist and Fellow of the American College of Nutrition based in Naples, Florida.

Dr. Perlmutter is recognized for addressing the root causes of neurological conditions and for identifying the underlying triggers of the patient's problems, thus practicing Functional Medicine. I downloaded the book on my iPad and read it that weekend. Later, I ordered a hard copy from Amazon. Grain Brain was the initiation of my education in nutrition and brain health. It was the first book in my Functional Medicine library.

For years, Dr. Perlmutter treated his neurological patients with prescribed medications with little success. However, when he changed their diets by removing gluten and adding healthy fats and certain vitamins, their symptoms improved and in some cases, disappeared altogether. His book discusses how gluten causes inflammation in the brain and is the cornerstone of many neurodegenerative diseases including Alzheimer's, MS, Parkinson's, and Rheumatoid Arthritis. According to Perlmutter, they are all fundamentally inflammatory diseases of the brain. He claims that the food we eat affects our neurological function and contributes to this inflammation. What an insight into the root cause of my illness and what an inspiring possibility to heal!

Grain Brain totally resonated with me. I suffered from food sensitivities for years. Dealing with this issue is highly complex as our bodies may not react to the foods we eat for up to seventy-two hours. How do you know which food or drinks caused the reaction?

In the mid-90s, I saw a French homeopath who attempted to sort out my digestion issues. He suggested eliminating many foods and taking tons of supplements and tinctures. It was a constant stress to think about what to eat, especially in restaurants or when traveling. There was never a definitive answer. It took so much discipline to live like that, and the problems always resurfaced. Eventually, I gave up.

Without realizing, I had been starving my body of the fuel it required to function properly, which resulted in malnourishment – exactly what the Long Island therapist had suggested the previous summer. My body had been robbed of the essential nutrients it needed to feed my brain. What a discovery!

Now, I was on to something that made sense to me. I knew there was not only hope to heal my body, but a way to do it. It was time to get serious and discover what foods and nutrients would benefit my body and which would be triggers for inflammation.

Around the same time, I downloaded "The Autoimmune Summit: Learn How to Prevent and Reverse Autoimmune Disease and Live the Long, Healthy Life You Deserve" hosted by Dr. Amy Myers, a Functional Medicine ER trained medical doctor in Austin Texas. It lasted for seven days and included thirty-eight interviews with experts discussing how to address the root causes of autoimmune conditions as well as prevention and reversal strategies. The goal was to allow participants the opportunity to "live the long, healthy life you deserve." Music to my ears.

Experts in the field of Functional Medicine and autoimmune disease explained how leaky gut, genetics, and environmental triggers such as toxins, food sensitivities, infections, and stress play a part in the development of autoimmunity. Some of the speakers from the summit made a huge impact on me. Specifically:

- Michael Ash, The Gut and Immune System Connection
- Dr. Alessio Fassano, The Role of Gut Permeability in Autoimmune Diseases: How to Distinguish Facts from Fiction
- Dr. Leo Galland, Understanding Triggers and Treatments for Inflammatory Bowel Disease
- Dr. Mark Hyman, A Functional Medicine Approach to Autoimmunity

- Dr. Alejandro Junger, How to Detox in the Modern World
- Dr. Frank Lipman, The Importance of Cleansing Your Body and Your Mind
- Dr. Amy Myers, The Autoimmune Solution: 5 Key Factors that Influence Autoimmunity
- Tom O'Bryan, The Gluten Autoimmune Connection
- Michael Kellman, The Microbiome Diet
- Dr. Martin Blaser, Missing Microbes
- Dr. David Perlmutter, The Brain, Gut and Autoimmunity
- and last but not least, Dr. Terry Wahls, Micronutrients, Macronutrients, Mitochondria and Autoimmunity and The Wahls Protocol

The seminar was geared toward professionals and thus was packed with difficult-to-follow medical terms. After listening for many hours, the language became more familiar and the overall concept of autoimmunity became much clearer to me. Once again, I enjoyed listening to a lively discussion of the latest scientific research. Many people shared personal stories of how conventional medicine had not healed them, but the discovery of Functional Medicine had been the key to renewed health and wellness.

Most importantly, I learned the " Five Environmental Factors that Contribute to Autoimmunity":

1. Gluten, grains, and diet
2. The gut
3. Toxins and detox
4. Stress and hormones
5. Infections

I read one book after another and devoured as much information as I could through blogs, articles, and podcasts. Every doctor referred to other doctors who focused on this new research. They cited landmark scientific studies that addressed inflammation and autoimmunity.

I learned about the microbiome and how 70 – 80% of our immune system is in the gut. All the research supported the idea that nutrition – the delivery and absorption of the necessary micronutrients – is the key to healing the body on a cellular level.

One of the books that had the greatest impact on me was The Wahls Protocol. In the book, Dr. Wahls shares her own incredible story of how she cured her MS through specific food choices and eliminations. In just one year, she went from being in a wheelchair to riding 18 miles on her bike. Her journey to wellness is an inspiration on healing the myelin sheath with proper nutrition.

Sadly, the Baltimore neurologist wasn't buying any of it. He rolled his eyes when I told him about my new diet. We discussed it one day after I had prepared a totally organic, nutritious, and delicious lunch at my apartment. I was feeling better – relatively speaking – but was still unable to get up from the chair without support and could not walk on my heels.

He told me I still had active CIDP and if I didn't want to take steroids then I should consider one of four chemotherapy drugs, which he wrote down. He cautioned there were "side effects" though and said, "You will probably get lymphoma but that's easy to cure." OMG, WTF? I was horrified. Instead, I said, "Why would I ever take chemotherapy drugs and risk getting cancer to cure an autoimmune disease, which on the whole is not that horrible?" I told him I would never take chemotherapy drugs under any circumstances. That put an end to the conversation and he abruptly left my apartment.

I was incensed that my doctor had suggested chemo as a viable treatment option, especially after I had just shared all I learned about healing through nutrition. We were not on the same page. Imagine my distress over this conversation with one of the world's experts in GBS/CIDP. And to think I was doing so well with my medical massages and the detoxifying teas! It had been five or six months without a trip to the hospital and I hadn't had steroids since December.

Despite our unpleasant conversation, the Baltimore neurologist and I stayed in touch. I was anxious about going to the contemporary auctions in London in June. It would be my first overseas trip since the diagnosis. I recalled my New York neurologist's words, "If your peripheral nervous system is going to heal, it will do so by the end of the first year. If not, it probably won't heal."

In the back of my mind, the one-year mark was my goal to feel well again and I was coming up on it. I was disheartened that, despite everything, my body was far from fully healed. The neuropathy and the weakness were still there. Without dwelling on it too long, I decided to switch gears and embrace Plan B, which always offers new possibilities and solutions. I said to myself, "Okay, perhaps it will take longer. No problem. I'll be patient."

Dr. Thomas Rau's book, The Swiss Secret to Optimal Health: Diet for Whole Body Healing, gave me new insights into how the body works. Dr. Rau is the medical director of the Paracelsus Clinic in Lustmühle, Switzerland. In his book, he stated:

"All organs regenerate themselves constantly. Our goal is to substitute healthy cells for weak or damaged cells. Providing the right nutrition helps create a healthier organ by establishing an optimal internal environment for at least one or more generation span of the organ's cells – that is, to replace all the cells in an organ with new and better cells takes at least as much time as the lifespan of those cells. It is because it takes about three weeks for the intestinal bacteria to turn over that my Swiss Detox Diet takes twenty-one days."

The book included a list of the life spans of various cells. At the bottom of that list was "nerves," which take two to seven years to regenerate, trailing behind bones, which take two to six years. From this information, I gathered that even though it may take two to seven years for the peripheral nervous system to regenerate, it was possible! This encouraged me to keep seeking information. I was hungry for studies and research that supported these theories.

Chapter Five
Summer 2014

June

A Grueling Trip to London, One Year Later

In early June, I scheduled an appointment with the neurologist at Johns Hopkins for a follow-up exam. The goal was for him to give me the go ahead to fly to London for a week to attend the auctions and bid on behalf of my clients. After six months without steroids, fueled by the detoxifying teas, and feeling a little stronger due to the medical messages, I easily managed to take the train to Baltimore on my own.

To save time during our appointment, I emailed him in advance to share what had been going on. The highlight was that I'd been gluten free since late April but still suffered from the neuropathy. He thought I was likely lacking important vitamins and recommended running various blood tests.

Surprisingly, the blood results came back fine. My vitamin D levels were very high, which I thought quite impossible after a long winter in New York without sun exposure. He examined me, conducted the usual strength tests, and pronounced I was fine and that I could do anything and go anywhere.

Despite this happy news, I still did not feel fine and knew I needed help to make the trip and asked Ben to join me in London. He would arrive the day after me and accompany me to the various events, exhibitions, and auctions together.

In advance of the trip, I packed a week's supply of teas in plastic bottles because I simply could not travel without them. Finding my seat on Virgin's sleep cabin was a challenge and I struggled to navigate the steps to the upper level of the plane with my carry-on bag. When the stewardess saw me, she immediately took the bag and helped me to the seat. She asked if I needed extra assistance when we landed, to which I said, "Of course not, I'm fine!" Wishful thinking.

After about five hours of sleep, I woke up and felt very strange, as if I had neuropathy throughout my whole body. It was not a sensation I had ever experienced before and it was frightening. Wondering if I would be able to walk off the plane, I summoned the stewardess over, explaining that I had a health issue, was feeling weird, and wasn't sure if I would be able to walk. She suggested that we arrange for a "chair" (as in wheelchair) to meet me at the plane and take me through Customs and Immigration when we landed. As the gate was at the farthest possible end of the terminal, I accepted the chair and was relieved to have the assistance.

All the while, I worried about what would happen if someone saw me that I knew and what I would say. Although I had shared my ordeal with close friends and family at the "coming out" party in April, I wasn't prepared to get into it with casual acquaintances from the art world. Thankfully, I didn't run into anyone while I was in the wheelchair and was able to retrieve my luggage and find the driver to take me into London.

Once at the hotel, I felt much better and walked over to Piccadilly to have breakfast. Later that day, I had difficulty getting out of a cab while holding my handbag. I worried, "Am I up to this trip? How will I manage these basic movements?"

Ben arrived late that night and in the morning we met up with my friends, Georgie and Johann, from Monte Carlo at Sotheby's. We decided to have lunch and do the rest of the day together, which entailed previewing the sales at the other auction houses and visits to the Saatchi gallery, White Cube Gallery on Bermondsey Street, and the sculpture exhibition at the Hayward within the Southbank Centre. We were gone all day long.

Georgie walked slowly and held onto Johann's arm for support, and I did the same with Ben, which made life easy! Up the stairs, down the stairs, and up the stairs again. We found elevators whenever we could, which I had never noticed before. We had a wonderful day enjoying contemporary art. It was especially enjoyable to have Ben accompany me. The trip went very well.

At the end of the week, I left for New York and Ben went on to Paris. On my way home, the gate was very near the Customs and Immigration and I had no problem walking there on my own, without any "assistance."

Feeling rather well upon my return, I decided it was time to go off the teas, massages, and trips to Connecticut to see how my body would feel. This decision was partly due to the therapist's refusal to tell me what was in the teas. She was paranoid that someone would steal her magic formula and recreate it on their own. Even after assuring her that I was not interested in making my own teas and that it was very important to know what was going into my body, she would not divulge the ingredients.

It was time to move on and see how I fared without her teas and magic touch. Of course, it was a worrisome decision, as I attributed the medical massages and teas to keeping me out of the hospital. On the one hand, I was pleased that I felt well enough to have made the trip to London, and on the other hand, I was still concerned about ongoing digestion problems and continued lack of energy.

On summer weekends, I stayed with my family and friends in the Hamptons and usually did well. One weekend, when I tried to swim in Darcie's pool, I only managed to swim the width of the pool instead of the length. The following day, I did ten lengths, struggling slowly the entire time. After lunch, I announced that I was going inside to rest for five minutes and wound up sleeping for two hours as I was totally exhausted and far from fine.

Another weekend, I had trouble getting out of the pool at Catherine's house. My legs felt heavy and my arms didn't have the strength to swim even one lap. I had to be helped out of the pool and was unable to manage the three little steps on my own, Not a good sign.

July

Out with Gluten, In with Organic

I continued reading about the brain-gut connection. Many of the experts from the Autoimmune Summit said gut health was the key to overall health because 70 – 80% of the immune system is in the gut. If my autoimmune disorder was caused by a weak immune system, then restoring my gut health would pave the way to get my energy back. It was time to deal with my gut in a new way and change my food intake. What marvelous medicine: to eat my way back to health. I was totally convinced that the gut was both the cause of my illness and an opportunity for a cure, and I was up for the task.

One day, I went into my kitchen and removed all of the food that contained gluten from the cabinets and the refrigerator. The next stop was the Westerly Health Market on 8th Avenue and 54th Street where I loaded up on all of the things on my very long list of organic and gluten free foods.

All of the books I'd been reading included simple recipes to plan and prepare nutritious and delicious meals. It was a big adjustment, but having the breakfast, lunch, and dinner recipes in front of me made it easier. I couldn't believe how much enjoyment I got from buying organic, fruits, vegetables, meats, fish, nuts, and seeds.

Even without gluten, I was able to eat a varied diet of raw salads, goat cheese and yogurt. For years, I'd been told to avoid eating raw vegetable salads because they are hard to digest. I realized how poorly I'd been eating for years and started to concentrate exclusively on eating the right foods including tons of mixed green salads with colored vegetables.

The trickiest part of my new nutritional regime was not eating in restaurants. Going out to eat was a big part of my life for years to meet my friends and clients. Under the new plan, I avoided making lunch and dinner dates and suggested we dine in my apartment instead. Everyone was shocked when I told them I cooked. The truth is, I enjoyed preparing nutritious meals and sharing them with my guests. I built up quite a repertoire of dishes that included beautiful raw salads, poached chicken breasts, baked wild salmon, wild cod and sautéed kobe beef sliders in coconut oil with tons of steamed vegetables. I omitted all bread, pasta, and desserts. Meal preparation was indeed a full time job.

While celebrating my birthday dinner at Le Bernardin with Darcie, Chris and Ben, the waiter asked if anyone at the table had any food allergies. There was no easy response but Chris had the answer. He suggested that I simply order everything grilled with the dressing on the side and no sauces. Skip the breadbasket and refrain from ordering desserts. This was great advice and it's precisely how I have handled ordering food in restaurants ever since.

August

Relapse

By mid-August, I was unable to walk up the stairs at Catherine's house one weekend and was noticeably weaker. I had to use the elevator to go upstairs to my room. I thought with deep frustration, "Oh no. Here we go again."

That evening, I joined my Baltimore neurologist and his wife at the Shabbat service at the Sag Harbor Synagogue. I was unable to get up from the chair without support and needed to hand the prayer book to him upon rising. We both knew it was not a good sign.

He suggested I make an appointment to see him in his office at Johns Hopkins the following week. By the time the appointment date arrived, I was unable to travel and could hardly walk. We decided that I should have another round of steroids and get checked out by the neurologist in New York, who would order the treatment and arrange to have it administered at home.

I was devastated but had to face the fact that I had relapsed. It wasn't easy to accept. I guess those detoxifying teas and medical massages in Connecticut had kept me out of the hospital after all!

The New York neurologist was surprised to see me. He said, "My goodness, it's been almost a year. That's a long time, but you look fine!" Nevertheless, he arranged for an at-home IVMP.

A few of the nurses that came to my apartment to administer the IVMP treatment were familiar to me from the previous year. I didn't get the initial kick that I had with the first "hit" in the hospital in October of 2013. This time, it took longer to feel stronger.

Over the next few weeks, I scheduled two or three medical massages a week with a masseuse in a nearby spa, barely being able to walk down the hall. It was much easier than going to Connecticut. I continued with the IVMP at home. After four treatments in four weeks, we tapered off to one week on and one week off and then I decided – that's it. No more!

The summer ended quietly. I had planned to spend the last few weeks visiting my family in Montreal and Ottawa as I had in years past, but unfortunately was unable to make the trip. My brother, Alan, was very upset. He told me on the phone, "You could do it if you wanted to." He knew I had been to London in June and out to Long Island most weekends in the summer. He thought I wasn't trying hard enough to see the family and became angry and impatient, which made me very upset! I got off the phone with him and cried my eyes out. I cried for his lack of understanding, but I also felt sorry for myself – for being weak again and for having to cancel all of the fun things we had planned.

After a good cry, I collected my thoughts and sent him an email. It said, "For the last year, I have been suffering and struggling to regain my health. I never know what each day will bring, or how my body will feel and what it will be able to do. All I need and want to hear is encouragement and not criticism." It made me feel better to write to him. He never replied, but I put the conversation behind me. From then on, we continued our wonderful relationship and I never heard another critical word from him again.

Chapter Six
Autumn 2014

September

Knocked Down in Chicago

Due to the steroid treatments, I felt stronger and booked a flight to Chicago for the Art Fair to attend the opening of Sarah Charlesworth's photography exhibition at the Art Institute. Chicago is an easy trip and I'd only be away for one night. Two years before, I had stayed for three nights, but that seemed like a lifetime ago.

While walking through the Chicago airport, I suddenly fell flat on my face. I was completely startled, lying on the floor. A young woman immediately came rushing over and apologized profusely. Apparently, she was wheeling her suitcase horizontally and it hit me from behind and knocked me over. She felt terrible and asked how I was, if I was hurt, if anything was broken. I was in shock and thought, "What did I break? A hip, an arm, a wrist, a knee?"

I got up with the help of a young man nearby. My knee was sore and achy as was my hand that tried to protect the fall. Nothing was broken though; what a relief. When I arrived at the hotel, I iced my swollen left knee and right hand, which were already turning black and blue, and rested. No real harm had been done, but the fall left me weaker and unstable.

Soldiering on, I attended the lecture and opening at the museum that night as scheduled. There was a lot of walking up and down stairs to get to my seat in the auditorium, and I needed to hold on to the rails. I declined dinner with a colleague and went straight back to the hotel to rest up for the VIP opening the next day.

In the morning, my knee was still swollen. I had to sit down at each booth with the gallery owners and explain that I was knocked over in the airport and needed to rest. My knee was aching. Putting cabbage leaves on the sore parts was the only thing that relieved the swelling and pain. It was a suggestion the massage therapist in Connecticut gave to all her patients who suffered from pain. Cabbage has anti-inflammatory properties and seems to do the trick every time.

Despite the fall, the trip to Chicago was a triumph. I succeeded in placing a stunning sculpture in a client's collection and spent the entire weekend back in New York negotiating on their behalf.

I was able to attend Serena's 6th birthday party in September. It was a joy to meet her new classmates and their parents from her kindergarten class at Chapin. Looking back to her 5th birthday when I was hospitalized caused me to realize how much progress I'd made despite the recent relapse.

October

In Search of the Root Cause

My strength slowly returned due to the steroid treatments, but I didn't feel well enough to go to London in October for the Frieze Art Fair or the FIAC in Paris the following week. I didn't have the stamina to walk or stand for long periods of time. The same old weakness and lack of energy continued to be a problem.

I was eager to focus on the next step, which was to find the root cause of the problem, get treated without steroids, and stay well. In my research, I discovered the Paracelsus Clinic in Switzerland, which practices biological medicine. The clinic is well known for searching for the root causes of illness, not merely treating the symptoms. A friend had experienced success there with a sick grandchild who had been treated for and cured of rheumatoid arthritis. The pain and symptoms disappeared and the girl was able to go off all of all of her meds. Perhaps I could experience the same success there. I emailed the clinic to learn what was involved and was fascinated by its various approaches, including genetic blood testing and checking dental inserts for mercury.

Instead of making the long trip to Zurich, which I really wasn't up to, I opted to have some tests done through the Center for Health and Healing, where I had been a patient since the practice opened in 2000. I made an appointment with my doctor and presented her with a list of tests from the clinic in Switzerland. She was unfamiliar with them and suggested I meet with an internist on their staff who practiced Functional Medicine.

The internist did not take on new patients unless she believed she could help their conditions. We had a brief chat on the phone and I made an appointment to see her the following week. During the appointment, she inquired about all sorts of childhood health issues. She wanted to know about my early adulthood in New York City and several other life matters that I had never connected with autoimmunity. She recommended a barrage of blood tests, including genetic testing, all of which were done in the office. She also ordered comprehensive digestive stool analyses, bacterial sensitivity, intestinal permeability and parasitology tests, which were done at home and sent to Genova Diagnostics in North Carolina via FedEx.

November

Test Results

When the test results came in, we met again to go over them. It was a fascinating visit and it gave me a whole new insight into (and language for) what was going on in my body and gut. For example, the tests revealed:

➤ I have one copy of the gene MTHFR, (methylenetetrahydrofolate reductase, A1298C variant), which slows my folate metabolism slightly.

➤ My homocysteine levels were high. Homocysteine is an amino acid made from a common dietary amino acid, methionine, that inflicts damage to the arterial lining (endothelium) and contributes to many diseases including cardiovascular, stroke, migraines, age-related macular degeneration, brain atrophy, and Alzheimer's.

➤ My DHEA (dehydroepiandrosterone) levels were very low. This is a hormone that comes from the adrenal gland. It is also made in the brain. DHEA levels decrease after age 30.

➢ The stool analysis showed a low level of a major beneficial bacterial group, bifidobacteria, and SIBO (small intestinal bacteria overgrowth).

The internist recommended a breath test (for SIBO: small intestinal bacteria overgrowth) with a gastroenterologist and Methyl CpG, which is a comprehensive formula that includes targeted amounts of five key nutrients to aggressively support methylation and homocysteine balance in the body. It provides a high concentration of folate and trimethylglycine to boost my B vitamin intake and compensate for the MTHFR gene being unable to produce adequate folate. Does that sound like Greek? It did to me too.

My research and study of the new terminology continued. Ever hopeful, I tended to think the mystery of my illness had finally been solved with each new doctor, practitioner, or book. My philosophy has always been to move on, don't blame anyone, and don't get discouraged; just keep moving forward. I was reminded once again of what Winston Churchill said: "Never, never, never give up! Keep on going from plan A to B." I was now ready to embrace Plan D (or was it E?).

When I shared the results of my latest doctor's visit with Ben, he listened and said, "Mom, you're always so excited with each new person you find. How is this doctor going to be any different than all the others?"

I told him that the possibility of healing in a new direction was exciting to me. It made me feel like I would be healthy again. When things don't work out, I'll move on to the next. I must acknowledge that every doctor, diagnosis, and treatment added to my knowledge of what to do and what not to do. I am grateful to everyone who treated me. They each contributed to the journey of reversing my autoimmunity.

Chapter Seven
Winter 2014 – 2015

December

Antibiotics Gone Awry

In early December, the art world gathers in Miami for Art Basel. In 2014, I stayed for four nights and felt happy to be well and able to stay twice as long as the year before. This was definitely progress! But to what did I owe my new-found wellness? It's an ongoing question: Was it the Methyl CpG supplement and the large dose of B vitamins? I was beginning to think it was.

Encouraged, I started the ball rolling for the SIBO breath test. First, I was required to meet with the gastroenterologist for a consult and then scheduled an appointment for the test the following week. He was eager to have me as a patient and I had to explain that I was only there for the SIBO breath test. Working with the new internist gave me renewed confidence and it's always complicated bringing another doctor into my long medical history.

The day before the test, Kara picked the lactulose up from the gastroenterologist's office downtown. The instructions were to fast from midnight on and to drink the lactulose one hour before the appointment. The test consisted of breathing into a cup every 15 minutes for a few hours, which eventually creates a pattern. It was non-invasive, but very time consuming, and as I later found out, not always accurate.

The results came in a few weeks later and showed a low level of SIBO. The gastroenterologist recommended that I take the antibiotic, Xifaxan, for 30 days. When I went over the results with the internist, I mentioned being concerned about taking antibiotics. She suggested taking saccharomyces boulardii, a probiotic to balance the antibiotic.

My new regime was one Methyl CpG tablet daily after breakfast, as well as the Xifaxan and saccharomyces boulardii. The cost of one month's supply of this antibiotic was $900. Eventually, my insurance covered a portion of the cost after several long hours on the phone negotiating it.

Once all the testing was complete and my new regime was underway, I emailed my Baltimore neurologist to give him an update on my health status.

The trip to Miami was a great success in terms of being able to travel on my own. Although, at times, it required a little arm support from my companions and getting off my feet for a few minutes to recharge.

I believe the CIDP has always been active, as I have never really felt normal or strong since the onset. The IVIG and IV MP treatments helped but only briefly.

My goal is to find the root cause of my autoimmunity. The Functional Medical community uses a different approach, which consists of the 3 pillars of autoimmunity:

1. Genetics
2. Environment (toxins, stress)
3. Gut dysbiosis (a term for a microbial imbalance)

Recently, I have undergone many blood tests and various stool analyses with an internist at the Center for Health and Healing, affiliated with Beth Israel Medical Center where my regular doctor practices. The results revealed various issues including:

1. Lack of digestive enzymes
2. 1 copy of the MTHFR gene
3. Overgrowth of bacteria in the small intestine (SIBO)
4. An imbalance of bifidobacterium in the gut

Currently, the treatment includes:

1. Xifaxan
2. Saccharomyces boullardi to counteract the Xifaxan
3. Methyl CpG
4. Vitamin D3

For decades, I wondered what enzyme was missing that did not allow me to digest food properly. Is it possible my body, unable to absorb the nutrients necessary for neuromuscular function, caused the onset of GBS and then CIDP?

My internist's plan is to attempt to remove the toxins, balance the gut, and retest after the above treatments at the end of the month and see where we are. This is the way I have chosen to go forward.

I am very grateful to you for all your assistance and being there for me. You have encouraged me to be well and live my life! Thank you!!

Best,

Linda

His response was:

While it is great that you feel better on the new diet, you should understand that there is no reason to think the diet will improve your CIDP. There is no published literature or clinical experience to suggest that these "immune" diets improve CIDP. Rather, there is both published data and extensive clinical experience on medications to treat your CIDP. I mentioned both azathioprine[2] and mycophenolate[3] as ones to consider but you would need a formal visit to move forward.

While you will make the ultimate decision, I would strongly recommend a visit with your New York neurologist, as he is closer, to quantitate you now and see where you go over time. I mentioned seeing if you could get off the sofa once the cushions are removed as one way to test yourself. Timing yourself by walking a known distance, say two blocks to the corner of Fifth Avenue and Central Park South, would be another. Recording these a few times/week would be helpful to see which direction you are going.

Let me know what you think.

---

[2] Azathioprine is an immunosuppressive medication. It may increase risk of developing certain types of cancer, especially skin and lymphoma. The drug is used to prevent the rejection of a transplanted kidney.
[3] Mycophenolate is an immunosuppresent drug used to prevent rejection in organ transplantation

Enjoy.

When I returned to the gastroenterologist after 30 days for a follow-up, the results were astonishing: my SIBO levels were 3X higher! He was suffering from the flu and sounded very unhealthy. He told me to take triple the dose of Xifaxan. My reply was, "With all due respect, doctor, if one daily dose of Xifaxan made the SIBO so much worse; what would three times the dose do? It doesn't seem to be effective for my body and I will not take any more. Thank you very much." And then I left his office.

January

Another Failed Procedure

I told the internist about the negative experience with the gastroenterologist when I saw her next. She recommended another doctor, a clinical professor of gastroenterology at Mt. Sinai, who she said was the SIBO expert. I made an appointment with him at the end of the month. The rigmarole with new doctors was becoming exhausting.

I looked and felt healthy and well during my first visit with the doctor from Mt. Sinai. He listened to my medical history and asked if I'd ever had a CT scan of my abdomen and pelvis, which I had not. He recommended it and as I was still in the "listening to the doctors" mode, made an appointment.

Before the abdominal, pelvic CT scan, I had to drink three large bottles of barium sulfate in the waiting room. I will not begin to describe what this did to my system, but when I got home from the hospital, my stomach was so upset I couldn't drink or eat anything for 24 hours. Somehow, I managed to keep my dinner date with Jerald at Porter's in the Time Warner Center that evening. I told him it would be the cheapest date ever because I couldn't eat or drink anything. As usual, he was a good sport about it.

During the follow up visit with the doctor a few days later, he told me the tests came back normal, as I expected. He said I had "fast transit" and suggested taking Imodium AD when necessary. Once again, I said, "With all due respect, doctor, I think that's what got me into trouble in the first place." He also suggested that I take a probiotic supplement called Align, which can be bought over the counter. That didn't work either, probably due to the additional synthetic ingredients, binders, and fillers. It also contained whitening titanium dioxide and other colorants, so obviously the bad ingredients outweighed the good!

The best take away from the internist was that she provided me a window into what was going on in my body, and I am forever grateful to have that knowledge. Her approach to the various tests to analyze my body was excellent, and the Methyl CpG vitamin helped tremendously. Unfortunately, both of her referrals proved to be very disappointing. I dumped a lot of harsh toxic medicine into my system without seeing any concrete improvements. In fact, they caused much distress to my body.

After the two failed gastroenterologist experiences, I decided to go it alone. No more doctors who suggested harsh tests and no more products that totally disturbed my delicate system. I would continue the search for the root causes on my own. I was ready to focus on Plan G. The next challenge was how to deal with the issues revealed through the testing.

Meanwhile, I had another distraction, but a good one this time! Ben was dating a woman he met a few months earlier. They planned to go to Miami for the long Martin Luther King weekend. Being the curious person that I am, I organized a ride down to Miami with my friends, Didi and Oscar, and stayed with their daughter, Alexis, at her apartment in South Beach. I texted Ben and said, "What a coincidence! I'm in Miami for the weekend and would love to meet Heather." Of course, Darcie advised me against contacting them and interfering in their getaway, but I couldn't help it.

The next day, Ben responded and invited me to meet him and Heather for a drink at the James Hotel on Saturday evening. Thrilled to have this opportunity, although walking unsteadily, I took a taxi to meet them. After five minutes in her company, I knew she was the one!

When I suggested they visit me on Fisher Island the next day, Heather said they would love to, but her parents were coming to Miami to have lunch with them. Aha! It was a "meet the parents" weekend. I knew she was serious about Ben too! We all waited to see how the relationship would develop. What a lovely distraction from all the recent doctor visits and tests. Ben and Heather were married in Williamsburg on May 20, 2017!

February

Heart to Heart with Darcie

Darcie and I speak almost daily. One morning, I mentioned that I'd been writing about my "ordeal." We talked about how surprisingly emotional it was for me to go over all of the details and events of the past months. Whenever Darcie asked, "Mom, how are you?" I always said "I'm fine," no matter how I was feeling. I preferred to hear what my wonderful granddaughters, Serena and Alessandra, were up to. I always enjoyed a good laugh hearing about the funny things they did and said. Who wants to hear their mother complain and whine about her ailments?

Darcie said it's important to acknowledge and express my feelings of sadness and worry. She said the only thing wrong with me was that I never acknowledged anything bad and always skipped to the good. She also said I never accepted the reality of my illness. As I listened to her, I knew she was absolutely right. I thoroughly agreed with her.

Heaving with emotion, I told her that always looking at the positive – no matter what I was told or read in the medical journals – was what had kept me going throughout all of the uncertainty and fear. Being positive was what kept me on the track to healing. On good days and bad days, I always had faith that I would be well again and regain my health. I never lost hope. Little did I know how much I would need this attitude in the months ahead.

Chapter Eight
Spring 2015

March

High Anxiety

It took about a month to regain my footing after the gastroenterology specialists. Although frustrated, I was determined to take matters into my own hands. A friend suggested contacting a well-known scientist in Santa Fe who had a PhD in nutritional biochemistry. There was a lot of homework to do in advance of talking with this person. It required completing a lengthy, twenty page confidential health history that included a comprehensive food dairy.

During my first consultation on the phone with him, we went over the questionnaire. He told me that my diet was very inflammatory. He recommended I follow the "O Diet" from Dr. D'Adamo's book, Eat Right for Your Blood Type, which I'd read twenty years earlier and it was still on my bookshelf in the kitchen. He sent me a list of foods to eat for breakfast, lunch, and dinner for a week.

After a few days on the "O Diet," my stomach was so distressed that I had to go back to my newly preferred diet of coconut oil, vegetables, salads, and organic meats. I felt better immediately. When we spoke the following week, the nutritionist told me I was an "outlier," meaning I fall outside of the norm. The term totally resonated with me. I was beginning to believe my whole system was an outlier. It was so easily upset by almost every product or meal plan that was suggested to me.

Following the blood type diet was just another step in the wrong direction. That research was twenty years old. Why did I listen to it? I was more attracted to the new research around the microbiome project anyway.

The scientist told me he was also a licensed psychologist. If I was willing, we could talk about my life and how it affected my health. Why not? We transitioned from talking about food and digestion to emotions and digestion. He cut to the chase and got me to open up about how I felt about many things, including being ill. I started crying on the phone with him and was very upset, but it felt extremely cathartic.

After a few more phone consults, I told him I was very happy in my life with my family, my friends and my career. I did not wish to continue our appointments, but he helped me to accept the fact that I was not perfect and my health was far from perfect. He gave me the courage to be less tough on myself, to share my situation (a little), and to ask for help when I needed it. This mindset was a big addition to my bag of healing tools.

I was finally able to be honest with myself about my condition and began to speak up when I needed assistance at the airport or when traveling. I also learned to acknowledge and express the fact that I was anxious about many things, and especially how my body would function on any given day. Would I be able to walk in the morning or after a long flight?

"Seniors" are often asked if they need assistance when booking flights or making travel arrangements. I started to answer "yes" and arranged for a wheelchair to take me to the gate and meet me at the plane upon arrival. If the gate was close to Customs and Immigration, I declined the chair and walked. Knowing someone would be there to meet me and help me get my luggage was very comforting and it relaxed me.

In addition to talking things through with the psychologist, I added various exercises the physical therapist at New York-Presbyterian Hospital/Weill Cornell Medical Center recommended. My morning routine included side leg lifts, calf raises, front leg lifts, calf stretches, squats, and lunges. In addition, I did balancing exercises on the bosu ball to help restore my balance. I also incorporated many exercises from The Wahls Protocol including hip lifts, back rolls, and various yoga stretches. Every other day I did upper body weights to build my strength.

My morning exercises became the barometer of how my body was functioning each day. Reducing inflammation in my body was directly related to how flexible I was on the floor and how easily my body moved. It was an enormous improvement from the time I could hardly sit on the floor or touch my toes. Excellent progress indeed.

April

How To Pace Myself

My health and strength improved steadily due to being able to talk about my anxieties, asking for help, eating healthy, and exercising daily. My goal since the autoimmune disease initially kicked in was to be well enough to celebrate renewed health with my friends in Italy at the end of May. The date was approaching and I faced the challenge of organizing the trip in a way that didn't incite another relapse. In the past two years, my longest trip has been a week in London. There were several other invitations and plans to consider as well.

The problem, or good news, was that I had a lot of choices and drove my assistant, Daniel, crazy with all the possible options, destinations, and connections. I was anxious about each step of the journey. How would I manage? Would I be able to do this trip? How would my body function? Logistics that had never crossed my mind in the past became critical considerations. Would there be stairs? How far away was everything? How long could I stand? What if I lost my balance?

Two years earlier, I wouldn't have given a trip of this length a second thought. Catching trains, moving luggage, and traveling long distances in short periods of time was second nature, but after my illness it was a different ballgame. I had to think about how my body will react every step of the way.

When I meditated about it, I was able to visualize how to approach the trip. It became clear to me how to plan it in a way that would protect my body from my very energetic brain. The key was to avoid early morning flights and those over seven hours long, which was the point at which the neuropathy worsened.

Happily, I discovered that wearing lace up sneakers allowed me to walk easily and steadily. This was a simple fix. I went to Nike and bought a pair of white, light leisure - not jogging - sneakers for my trip. I also found two pairs of flats that were comfortable to walk in: one black pair for evening and one beige pair for day. That took care of that.

After much debate, Daniel and I decided to organize the trip with as much ease of travel as possible. There would be no hectic art schedules on this trip and five spa days were scheduled in between major events.

May

France, Italy, and Israel

The trip began in Paris, where I met Jerald for four days before flying to Italy. We had planned the previous fall to visit the newly opened Fondation Louis Vuitton Museum in the Bois de Bologne. The Frank Gehry designed building for Mr. Bernard Arnault was stunning and the inaugural exhibition superb. We also took in the newly renovated Picasso Museum in the Hotel Sale in the Marais district as well as the various galleries in the area.

Since we were on our own schedule, we did everything at a leisurely pace and stopped when we needed to rest. We enjoyed delicious lunches and excellent dinners in the evening. It was a glorious start to my first long trip in years.

After a short flight to Florence, I was driven to Castiglion Del Bosco, a luxurious retreat in the heart of Tuscany to spend three wonderful days at a birthday celebration with friends. There was no hiking or walking for me, but I managed a few laps in the pool at Villa Costello, home to Mr. Salvatore Ferragamo when he is in residence. Some of the other guests and I were fortunate enough to stay there. My body felt lighter and my muscles cooperated in the pool.

One day, we ventured into the town of Pienza, which is situated between Montepulciano and Montalcino. It was my third visit to this charming town, which boasts superb Renaissance architecture. We all enjoyed the spectacular Cathedral Tower, the Palazzo Piccolomini on the square, and the beautiful views of the hills of Val d'Orcia while having our lunch al fresco. It was both magical and romantic to be in such a harmonious area of Tuscany.

That evening, dinner was at the Il Palazzone Winery in Montalcino, al fresco once again. The final dinner of the weekend was at Campo del Drago followed by dancing in the Villa Castello. It was a fun filled, stunning, and very late evening. I was thrilled and grateful to have been healthy enough to be a part of it.

After the fabulous weekend in Montalcino, I was driven to my hotel in Rome. I didn't have to stress about getting to the airport, making a connection, or waiting in long lines. After lunch on the terrace of my hotel overlooking the Spanish steps, I had the energy to hit the Maxxi Museum for an hour.

Because I had a morning flight to Tel Aviv the next day, I enjoyed a quiet and early night while still thinking of the wonderful weekend.

All of the stress and chaos of the airport in Rome was eliminated by arranging for a wheelchair in advance. There was no way I could have managed the Rome airport on my own. In Tel Aviv, I was met by a special custom's agent and then driven to Haifa and the Yarot Hacarmel Spa in the beautiful Carmel forest. I was in heaven. It was beautiful, peaceful, and the food was healthy and abundant. It seemed to be just what the doctor ordered (may I remind you that I AM NOW THE DOCTOR): early to bed, lots of sunshine, yoga classes, swimming and daily massages, as well as visits with my relatives, Debbie, Ronen and Shlomi, who live nearby.

For months, my friend Grete had encouraged me to join her and Hanno in Jerusalem for the 50th Anniversary of the Israel Museum. Because I had prioritized the June events, Israel was the next stop on the itinerary. On the first day, the International Council Program offered a walking tour of the Old City, which I happily joined, equipped with a hat, sun block, and sneakers. The tour involved a lot of walking and climbing on the cobblestones to see the ancient sites including the Western Wall, Church of the Holy Sepulchre, and the Jewish Quarter – home of the famous Shuk where people bustled and sold their wares. It is unquestionably one of the most intense places on earth.

The next few days were busy at the Israel Museum with tours of the new wings and exhibitions, lunches in the Rose Art Garden, a gala dinner and a surprise venue dinner the last evening followed by spirited dancing. It was a joy to have been well enough to enjoy five exciting days and it was thrill to be in Israel after so many years with many friends.

On my return to New York, I flew from Tel Aviv to London and spent the night at an airport hotel in Heathrow. The next day, I flew from London to New York and avoided a 13-hour flight from Israel. Breaking up the trip gave me the rest I needed and adequate sleep the night before an easy day flight home. By envisioning each step of the three-week trip, planning and scheduling for rest and relaxation, I was able to maintain my strength the entire time. Thank you, Dr. Silverman, for your advice!

Chapter Nine
Summer 2015

June

Walking in Central Park After Two Years

Back in New York, I continued to feel well. My next goal was to meet Didi in Central Park to resume our 8 am walks, which I was unable to do for the last two years. Once again, there was anxiety wondering how far I could walk and how would I feel afterwards.

Didi was thrilled and told me we'd take it easy. It was heaven to be back in the park, in nature, walking the paths. I needed to sit down and take a break on a bench after about 30 minutes but then I was good to go again.

After a couple of weeks, I was up for an hour, then one and a half hours, and then almost two hours without taking a break. It was easy to keep walking and talking as we always lost track of time. We enjoyed covering all the news topics of the day and exchanging our ideas for possible solutions.

At first, when returning from walking in the park with my friends, I sat in a chair and rested with my feet up for thirty minutes. Soon after, only a few minutes of rest was necessary. It was always a challenge to find the balance between pushing myself to do more when I felt well and stopping before losing ground. Perhaps those two-hour walks were a bit much, but the girls seemed to have forgotten that I hadn't been up to walking for a long time, since May 31, 2013.

Our walks took us briskly up the paths into the Rambles. We sat and chatted with Armando, who was always stationed on the same bench, with this box he beautifully painted with the words "The Power of Now, Eckhart Tolle". We watched him give treats to the dogs, as they often tried to chase the squirrels up the trees without any success. We fed the birds with seeds that they masterfully plucked from our palms. What a delicious feeling... Sitting on Armando's bench was a delight, an ever-changing dialogue with nature and a recharge for the rest of the walk home.

July

Getting Stronger

One of my primary health goals was to build up my physical strength. The walking certainly helped my legs. In order to strengthen my hands, I used therapy hand balls, which made a big difference. I no longer had trouble opening jars, using hairspray, or using my keys to unlock my apartment door. My body almost felt "normal" when I did my morning yoga stretches. I knew it was due to lowering the inflammation in my body, which is a key factor in reclaiming my health.

August

Reaching out to Beth Mosher, Complete Nutrition and Wellness Center

In mid-August, I reached the one-year mark without a relapse or the need for steroids. As you can imagine, I was thrilled, relieved, and encouraged to stay on my own course of healing with micronutrient rich foods, increased exercise, and lifestyle changes.

The next step was to address the ongoing challenge of my "food intolerances." According to the Autoimmune Wellness site:

> "Intolerances are milder than food allergies but have a cumulative effect of provoking the immune system and increasing inflammation in the body. If you have autoimmune disease, food intolerances exacerbate your symptoms, making them much worse. As food intolerance reactions are delayed and may take up to seventy-two hours to appear, it is highly problematic to figure out which foods are at fault."

In my research, I discovered the Alcat tests, which measure food sensitivities. Unfortunately, they were not performed in New York State. Through Cell Laboratories and several phone calls, I found the Complete Nutrition and Wellness Center in Hoboken, NJ that could perform this test. After setting up an appointment, I bravely took the Path train to Hoboken on a very humid, 90-degree day and found a taxi from the station to the Center.

The office was lovely, fresh and run by two healthy looking practitioners. My appointment was with Beth Mosher, a certified nutritionist, who had a Master's Degree of Science in Human Nutrition. She asked several informed questions based on my completed questionnaire and she had reviewed the many test results from the internist in advance of our appointment.

We quickly moved into a discussion about the microbiome and the theory of molecular mimicry. She explained how inflammation in the gut can affect the overall health of the body and impact the body's ability to heal. Beth also talked about nutritional biochemistry, genetics, neurons, and individual reactions. She did not talk about illness, pharmaceuticals, or hospitalization. We focused on nutrition and supplementation, which would help reduce inflammation and increase nutrient absorption to improve overall health.

My conversation with Beth restored my hope in a path to healing. All the while, though, Ben's question was going through my mind: Is this person really going to make a difference for me? Can she help me figure out what my body requires to be well and stay well? After all the doctors I had seen in the past two years, I wondered if I found the person who could provide the keys to reverse my health issues. Her approach certainly resonated for me.

She helped me to understand the test results from the internist. Beth explained that the elevated bilirubin in my blood work was an indication of a slowed phase II liver detoxification pathway called glucuronidation. People with this situation, she said, are often more chemical sensitive. This explained why I had such strong reactions to second hand smoke, cigar smoke and fresh paint which could cause acute headaches for days.

Beth's interpretation of my test results and genetics echoed the research I had done independently. All of the Functional Medicine books, podcasts, and webinars I consumed fell directly in line with her approach to healing. Therefore, it was easy for me to believe in it and follow her suggestions. I knew they would work and she knew I would do whatever it took to restore my health. She was pleased to have my feedback after changing certain foods or adding certain supplements. I told her I wanted to be alive to see my granddaughters marry and have children and see to what extent the robots invaded our lives. I'd always been fascinated by the future and how I would fit into it.

Finding Beth enabled me to advance my healing process using methods I believed in. I couldn't get enough of her explanations and Googled every word that I didn't understand. As I have no biology or chemistry background, it was very challenging to understand the science of the body, but I was fascinated to learn about biochemistry and how it affects health. I had finally found someone to work with who believed illness could be reversed through nourishing the body with food and supplements. This belief is the core of Functional Medicine.

Chapter Ten: Autumn 2015

September

The Evolution of Medicine: James Maskell

On Serena's 7th birthday, two years after I had been hospitalized, I was on the plane to LA to attend the opening of the Broad Art Museum. Before leaving, I texted Chris and asked him to look up to my living room window before Serena got on the school bus. When they walked out the front door, I opened the window, and called out, "Happy Birthday, Serena! I love you," and held up seven fingers. She loved it and happily hopped on the bus. I would miss her birthday party at the American Girl store, but I was looking forward to three wonderful art-filled days celebrating the opening of the Broad.

Daniel, my assistant, met me at the Ace Hotel in downtown LA. We had a quick snack and got an Uber to Beverly Hills for a cocktail reception at the home of Susie and David. It was a superb collection and I enjoyed seeing many works of art from David's parent's collection that I recognized from my Sotheby's days. They were among the early collectors of contemporary art along with the Broads.

The next morning, I was delighted to feel fine and we drove to Malibu to visit Marla's exquisite home and emerging art collection. After lunch outside at the Malibu Beach Inn, we went to MOCA for a tour of the collection and visited the Geffen Wing to see the Matthew Barney exhibit. I was feeling tired after so much walking and needed to sit down. As usual, I was anxious if this schedule was pushing myself too much. It was frightening how quickly jet lag and a long day of walking could slow me down. We opted for a quiet dinner outside at the hotel restaurant and had a relatively early night.

The next morning, we went to the Los Angeles County Museum of Art for a private view of Frank Gehry's retrospective exhibition. Afterwards, we visited the Gagosian Gallery to see the Urs Fischer Fountains and then went out to lunch. It felt good to sit down, enjoy a healthy meal, and recharge my system. In the afternoon, we headed to the Ovitz collection. There was a lot of walking, up and down stairs, and back to the car. Then, we returned to the hotel to relax before the Broad Art Museum Gala.

I thought about what shoes to wear with my silver silk jacket and pants outfit – the silver jeweled heels or the more practical black flats, which I knew would be more comfortable. Comfort won out. It had been over two years since I wore high heels. I was still waiting for the time when I could wear them again and know that my feet would feel fine and that my balance would be steady all evening. I wasn't quite there yet, maybe soon.

The evening was superb. There was lots of standing, walking around the stunning museum and viewing the exciting contemporary collection. Afterwards, everyone walked on the red carpet to attend the gala dinner and enjoy the entertainment. Having Daniel as my date made the evening (and the whole trip) much more relaxing and comfortable. It was an exciting event to be a part of and I was thrilled to be there with the Broads, who I knew when they had three works of art in their collection.

I arrived home late in the evening and set my alarm to wake up in time to walk in the park with Didi. With another trip under my belt, I was happy to still feel well and strong.

Always educating myself on new approaches to healing, I followed several sites on the topic. I received an email invitation to register for the second annual "Evolution of

Medicine Summit: Building Healthcare from Scratch"[4] hosted by James Maskell, the author of Evolution of Medicine and founder of the Functional Forum. When I clicked to register, there was a video presentation outlining the line up of doctors and researchers who would present over eight days.[5] Many of them were familiar to me and some were totally new.

The goals of the online summit were to advance and incorporate the practice of Functional Medicine into mainstream medicine and to motivate patients to become active participants in preventive care and recovery from illness with nutrition, lifestyle changes, exercise, and positive thinking.

Special guests included:

- Dr. Rangan Chatterjee, GP, BBC 1's Host Doctor in the House
- Dr. Kelly Brogan, Holistic Psychiatry, Women's Medicine

---

[4]http://abwellness.life/wp-content/uploads/2015/09/Rationale-for-HealthCare-from-Scatch-keynote-James_Maskell.pdf
[5] https://www.youtube.com/watch?v=ZQtyMTEfzLY

- Dr. Gerry Curatola, Biological Dentist, Host of the Dr. Gerry show on PBS
- Dr. Shilpa Saxena, Physician, Creator of Functional Medicine Group Visit Model

Among the most inspiring presenters on the panel was Dr. David Perlmutter, who wrote Grain Brain (2013) and Brain Makeover (2015). As I mentioned earlier, Grain Brain provided my first insight into Functional Medicine and how what we eat influences our health. A neurologist and fellow of the American College of Nutrition in Naples, FL, Dr. Perlmutter focused on gluten and its neurological impact and the relationship between diet and illness.

During his presentation at the Evolution of Medicine Summit, Dr. Perlmutter explained how inflammation and inflammatory diseases are influenced by gut bacteria. He said that most doctors never pay attention to what causes various neurological symptoms and they certainly never talk about nutrition. Sugar and carbs are the big culprits that lead us off the track. Specifically, grains are toxic to humans and cause inflammation. Good, natural fats are necessary for the brain and our DNA communicates with the food we eat and thus affects our health.

Perlmutter's revolutionary good fat diet is contrary to the low fat/high carb diet that the National Institutes of Health[6] was touting. Look where the low fat/high carb way of eating got us: obesity, diabetes, heart disease, Alzheimer's, and chronic inflammatory autoimmune diseases.

He quoted Hipprocates, the 4th Century BC Greek physician, "Let medicine be thy food and food thy medicine." He also said, "for those who care to listen, there is an answer out there for you!" I must say I was inspired. His words encouraged me to stay on my course of healing with Beth.

A vast wealth of cutting-edge information about the root causes of autoimmunity disorders is online for anyone who chooses to access it. Without the Internet, I never would have had exposure to the Functional Medicine community and its findings or known which path to follow to reverse my autoimmunity issues.

The top two neurologists from two of the finest hospitals in the country were not even up to date with this research. Their solution was drugs and more drugs, which are just a

---

6
https://www.nih.gov/news-events/news-releases/nih-study-finds-cutting-dietary-fat-reduces-body-fat-more-cutting-carbs

Band-Aid, or a temporary fix at best. My endless curiosity and unwavering will to be well is what enabled me to forge ahead in the search for the root cause of my illness.

The overall consensus among Functional Medicine experts who treat patients with autoimmunity is to recommend the total elimination of gluten from the diet. I had already taken that step a year earlier and saw a huge improvement in my body. At the onset of my illness, the soles of my feet were burning hot. They looked red and felt inflamed. Those symptoms completely disappeared when I removed gluten from my diet and my feet almost felt normal again. My Baltimore neurologist said this meant the nerve fibers in my body were healing. Yes!

For years, I thought I was eating a healthy diet, but it consisted of gluten-laden foods such as cereals, muffins, pasta, and tons of rye and wheat bread. I never had raw salads or adequate amounts of vegetables or essential fatty acids.

After the visit to my nutritionist in September and several follow-up telephone consultations, my diet changed again. Beth interpreted my genetics and test results to determine what was beneficial to eat and what was not. She was able to devise a food and supplement plan to compensate for the genes that did not function optimally. Her specific, targeted, individualized approach was the key to regaining my health.

My personal protocol based on my genes and tests was to eat more protein and more good fats. It required consuming incredible amounts of micronutrients, foods rich in essential fatty acids, B vitamins, and avoiding gluten and other foods that cause inflammation. Soon after I made these adjustments, I began to enjoy renewed energy and stamina.

October

Frieze Art Fair London

Having meticulously planned and thoroughly enjoyed my three-week international trip in May/June and returned in fine health, I began making plans to go to London for the Frieze Art Fair. As was my new custom, I fiercely guarded my health when reviewing the VIP invitations for the week and the schedule for FIAC in Paris the following week. To maintain my improved energy and prevent a relapse, I decided to go to London for six days and five nights only and skip Paris.

On the way to the airport, I texted Darcie and recalled that two years prior, I was in the hospital at my lowest point. It was four months after the GBS diagnosis and I struggled to walk with two canes, was on steroids, feeling hyper, weak and barely functioning. Now, I was heading to London (or Londoom, as Serena and Alessandra call it) to work, with a fully packed schedule to boot that started the minute I got off the plane. I was deeply grateful for my renewed health and independence, plus the ability to resume my life and travel schedule.

After several hours of sleep on the plane, I arrived at Heathrow. A wheelchair attendant met me at the gate and assisted me all the way through the terminal to retrieve my luggage and get transportation into the city.

My schedule began immediately after the bags were dropped off at the hotel desk. My friend Evie met me at the hotel and we walked to Cecconi's for an early lunch with my friend Joanie. It was a sunny day and I was happy to enjoy a lovely meal with two lovely ladies. Afterwards, we headed to the Royal Academy to see the Ai Weiwei exhibition, which was brilliant, followed by the Edmond de Waal exhibit. We continued on to Christie's to view the contemporary sale and then walked to Dover Street to see the preview of the Marion Lambert collection. What a day!

I started to get tired and headed back to the hotel to unpack, shower, and go to bed. After sleeping almost twelve hours and skipping the Tate Britain breakfast for the Waddesdon Manor exhibit, I felt totally refreshed. My medical research taught me that plenty of sleep was a key component in healing. It was critical for me to sustain my renewed strength and energy to prevent weakening or relapse. I did my exercises in my hotel room, had a healthy breakfast, and was ready to start the day at 11 am.

I met up with Evie to go to Sotheby's around the corner to view the contemporary works in the upcoming auction. Next it was off to Gagosian to see the new exquisite gallery with the beautiful Twomblys. We took a taxi to the ICA for lunch and previewed the Zhang Ding exhibit, which was very crowded, but the food was healthy and delicious. From there, we went to DRAF (David Roberts Art Foundation) and had a tour of the current collection and then off to view Jon Rafman at Zabludowicz. We decided to continue directly to the White Cube party at Bermondsey. I remember thinking that if I were in New York, I would never consider leaving the apartment in the morning and staying out until the end of the evening. I always built in time to go home, change and relax before going out again. Not so in London, where I was scheduled for morning through nighttime activities the entire week.

Having Evie to accompany me everywhere was such a delight and a comfort. She often grabbed my arm when we were walking and it felt very supportive. The art fair was much easier to navigate with a friend. There was a lot of walking and standing, but I was fine going from booth to booth to find works of art for my clients.

The decision to spend five days in London for Frieze and skip Paris for the FIAC was a good one. Darcie always said the reason I became ill was due to the non-stop traveling over the last several years. She had a good point. When I got my energy and health back, I started to limit my trips and be careful not to tire myself out. It definitely worked.

Being mindful of what I ate was paramount as well. By asking for the foods I wished to eat and not accepting what was on the menu, I was able to sustain my energy and feed my brain so my body functioned properly. I was no longer bashful about requesting food be prepared a certain way: no gluten, no dairy, no dressing (only olive oil and lemon), and always sauce on the side, as per Chris's advice many months earlier. Eating grilled fish, chicken, extra vegetables, and lots of avocados enabled me to stick to my plan and feel well.

In addition, I made time to do my exercises, stretch and meditate every day. A calm morning routine was a big factor in being able to maintain a busy pace. Sleep, healthy foods, and regular exercise, were the ingredients to maintaining my stamina. Also, Evie's companionship made the London trip seamless.

November

A Family Thanksgiving Getaway

The month of November is a hectic one in the art world. It's filled with previews, several contemporary art evening and day auctions, and many gallery openings. I paced myself to keep up with personal invitations, my clients, the art market, and my health.

When the month drew to a close, I wound down the sales and looked forward to spending Thanksgiving with Darcie, Chris, and the girls in Sagaponack. Ben would not join us that year. He was going to spend the holiday with Heather's family in Delray Beach. We had marvelous spring-like weather and were able to spend lots of time outdoors. Chris cooked a delicious turkey while Darcie and the girls prepared the side dishes.

It was truly a glorious, quiet and relaxing time; Serena and Alessandra dove into my bed every morning and I felt so healthy in the country. Although my mind was happier in the city, my body was so much happier in nature. The stress of the city evaporated immediately.

Chapter Eleven
Winter 2015 - 2016

December

The Year in Review

After a long telephone consultation with Beth, I added another supplement to my regime: Ultimate Flora Probiotic. In the past, I'd had conversations with other practitioners about probiotics but they were vague and confusing. The advice I received wasn't connected to my microbiome, and the various probiotics I tried never made me feel better. In fact, they made me feel worse so I stopped taking them. This time, with precise knowledge of what my body was lacking, I was finally able to take the right one, it agreed with me, and increased the good bacteria in my gut.

In order to know which probiotic to take, it was necessary to do specific stool analysis tests. They examined the types of bacteria that resided in my gut as well as inflammatory markers and the overall health of the colon. Beth explained that by balancing the gut bacteria and reducing inflammatory triggers in my diet, my digestion would improve. I started to wonder if it was possible that my body had started to attack itself (in the peripheral nervous system) because of the imbalance of bacteria in my gut?

Beth also informed me that I was not getting enough protein. She suggested that I eat protein, carbs, and good fat at each meal. My new breakfast consisted of two organic poached eggs, two pieces of nitrite-free organic turkey bacon, two pieces gluten-free bread toasted with organic ghee butter, 1/2 avocado, and decaf green tea. It's filled with good fats and fuels my brain, which is what my peripheral nervous system requires to function properly. Sometimes, I started with gluten-free oatmeal, fruit, a dash of ginger, and one tablespoon of flax oil before my morning walk. Both options kept me full all morning!

December always means Art Basel/Miami Beach and my schedule was packed, as usual. The trip down to Florida was easy. No assistance required at the airport and I stayed with my friend, Alejandra, on the beach. My assistant Daniel ordered my special food from Whole Foods: organic eggs, greens, vegetables, fruits, gluten-free bread, almond milk, and almond butter. It made eating healthy a breeze. The order was delivered shortly after I arrived.

After unpacking, I headed to the beach for thirty minutes to sit in the afternoon sun and gaze at the seagulls flitting in and out of the ocean. This brief time on the beach made me feel totally renewed, and I decided to spend more weekends in Florida in the winter. The vitamin D from the sunshine does wonders to the body. It was my only time to relax for the rest of the week. The schedule was more hectic than usual, but I was totally up to it.

After my return from Miami, there was an irresistible invitation in the mail. It was from Thaddaeus Ropac for a private viewing of Anselm Kiefer's exhibition at the Pompidou Museum in Paris with a dinner following in the artist's presence at Restaurant Theatre du Renard. Kiefer is one of my favorite artists. I had been pacing myself and felt fine but was worried about overdoing it. The invitation was too good to pass up and my friend, Annick, invited me to stay with her.

Paris was very sad, gray, and empty a month after the attacks in November. There were no tourists and the shops were vacant. On the first day, after lunch we headed to the Palais de Tokyo Museum to see a number of emerging artists including a timely super video by Vidali about migration, climate change, and the transformation of the world's population. We loved it.

That night, the traffic outside my window was annoying and I didn't sleep well. Perhaps, the jet lag caught up with me. I did not feel great the next day either and wondered how I would have the energy for the opening and dinner that evening. After a short nap and a healthy snack, I felt refreshed again and off we went in the pouring rain to the Pompidou. It was a fabulous thirty year retrospective and a wonderful dinner with fascinating and famous guests. The next morning, I woke up rested and ready for the journey back home.

It was easy to manage the trip to the airport on my own. Unfortunately, the Uber driver left me at Orly Sud and I had to take the tram with my bag to Orly Oeust. Transferring from one airport to another took some time, but I did it with ease and never felt like I needed any help.

On the plane, I watched an intriguing movie called On the Tour. It was about an interview with the author David Foster Wallace and a journalist from Rolling Stone magazine, played by Jesse Eisenberg. Throughout the entire movie, the two men ate the most disgusting junk. I couldn't help thinking perhaps binging on garbage food contributed to Wallace's mental problems and eventual suicide.

As 2015 came to an end, I looked back at the year and reflected on my progress since being diagnosed with Guillain-Barré syndrome in 2013. I realized how lucky I was to have been diagnosed and treated within twelve days of the first symptoms. It was truly a miracle to restore my health and well being to the extent that I had been able to. I couldn't do everything, but was able to prioritize the things I wished to do and enjoyed doing them.

It was important to monitor my progress as my body healed from the disease. My peripheral nervous system was damaged but little by little, things returned to normal. I was hopeful for a complete recovery and motivated to continue following the right protocols for my body.

During one of the presentations I saw on toxicity and autoimmunity, I discovered that most of the cosmetic products and creams I used were loaded with toxic chemicals. It never occurred to me how many chemicals get into our bodies through make-up, body and face creams, nail polish, shampoo, hairspray, sunscreens, and cleaning sprays. Gradually, I switched to non-toxic cosmetics and cleaning products from the health store.

Slowly, my life returned to "normal." The three-week trip to Europe and Israel in May/June set the stage to resume my morning walks in Central Park with Didi, Carolyn, and Lyanne. It took many walks, weeks, and months to build up my strength, but it was an exhilarating accomplishment to walk in the park again.

The combination of simple daily exercises for my feet, calves, quads, and hamstrings combined with stretching and weights was a key factor in building my strength. The body has the ability to become stronger and healthier when it is given what it needs.

The path to healing my body was multifold. I took it one day at a time, and tried to balance my schedule with all of the knowledge acquired from listening to online podcasts, as well as reading various Functional Medicine doctors/practitioners books.

Healing begins with the search for the root causes of illness, not the quick fix of pharmaceuticals. The IVIG and IV MP regime set me on the course of recovery initially, but the beneficial results were short lived. Eventually, they were more harmful than helpful to my body. I always knew there had to be a reason my body broke down and I was convinced that I could find out what it was and be well again. I was too young to degenerate in my 60s and be wheelchair bound. My faith to heal never wavered even once.

January

The Secret World Inside You

For almost a year, the American Museum of Natural History hosted an extraordinary special exhibition entitled "The Secret World Inside You,"[7] which I took Serena to see one Sunday. It was geared for children as well as adults. The entire show was about the microbiome, which consists of over 100 trillion tiny microorganisms that travel through the intestines and to keep us healthy. The exhibition's program said, "In 'The Secret World Inside You' you'll be introduced to the community of creatures that your immune system, digestive system, and brain rely on every day!" It led me to believe the scientific community was well ahead of the medical community, which had a long way to go to catch up.

It was fascinating to watch Serena react to the interactive activities and videos. She was deeply engaged in one of several pinball machine games. As the game began, three images of food appeared on the screen. For example, french

---

7

http://www.amnh.org/calendar/the-secret-world-inside-you

fries, ice cream and broccoli. When you clicked on them and pushed the lever, the food items were directed into the gut and you could see the results immediately. If the participant chose healthy foods (garlic, onions, apples, greens, carrots, etc.) they got a high score. A lower score indicated a choice of sugary bad foods. It was a quick, visual lesson in how to eat well for your microbiome and be healthy.

We learned there is a need for a huge diversity of bacteria to balance the immune system, 70-80% of which is in our gut. This fact alone represents a total shift in the overall view of what makes us ill or keeps us healthy. One of the most mind-blowing concepts was that the trillions of bacteria in our guts have the ability to turn our genes on and off. There are 22,000 genes and many trillions of bacteria. Bacteria are the drivers of our health, not the enemy.

Scientists involved with the microbiome research believe medicine will be practiced in an entirely new manner in the future. There will be an increased emphasis on eating food that feeds our bacteria and the consequences of overusing antibiotics. The message was universal for autoimmunity and many other illnesses.

The exhibit highlighted the five key ingredients to healing the body and staying healthy, which (not by coincidence) are the same four steps to achieving SuperBalance:

1. Nutrition: healthy foods that agree with one's genetics
2. Sleep: 8 hours
3. Stress: reduce stress and change lifestyle and relationships as necessary
4. Exercise: daily, outdoors if possible

February

WTF Should I Eat?

A few months after we started working together, Beth suggested that I try removing high salicylate foods from my diet to see if my digestion would improve even more. I had never heard the word salicylate before. Salicylates are natural chemicals in plant foods. Many people who are sensitive to sulfites are also sensitive to salicylates.

Curious, I downloaded a research paper called the Feingold Diet and discovered most of my food intake was on the high or very high salicylate list. This was a huge development on my path to healing. One of the main reasons I went to see Beth in the first place was because I needed help to figure out what foods were problematic and what foods were fine for my digestive system. The salicylate sensitivity added a whole new level of understanding to my nutrition and overall well being. It turned out that I had been eating a lot of foods I thought were good for me but due to this specific sensitivity, they were not.

Purposely, I consumed large quantities of high salicylate foods, or foods high in sulphur, such as spinach, kale, broccoli, almond milk, and cinnamon. I chose those foods based on *The Wahls Protocol* for reversing MS. I assumed that this diet would help other autoimmune diseases as well.

Through working with Beth, I realized that people should not listen to what other people eat without first knowing what's going on in their own bodies. This was perhaps one of the most important lessons I learned: there is no such thing as a one size fits all treatment plan (or pill, or dose of steroids, or diet). Everyone is unique, their microbiome is unique, and the foods or medicines that work or don't work for one person will not necessarily perform the same way for another.

As enlightening as this information was, once again, I had to find new foods to eat – the story of my life! At first, I was annoyed to have to study the research and make adjustments. It reminded me of an interview I watched with Dr. Mark Hyman who jokingly said he was going to call his next book, *WTF Should I Eat?* I could certainly relate!

With my eye on the ball, I reminded myself that the goal was to learn what to eat that agreed with my system. Following the Salicylate list and Beth's recommendations, I made a new shopping list, hit the health food store and bought many new foods. I also removed all of the high salicylate foods, herbs, and spices that irritated my gut from the refrigerator and cabinets. It was much easier to be mindful of what I put into my body when I thought about increasing good or decreasing bad bacteria for my specific system. If everyone ate according to our individual bacterial needs, the entire pharmaceutical industry would be out of business!

I replaced almond milk with cashew milk and almond butter with cashew butter. I continued using coconut milk for my smoothies but replaced spinach and kale with mixed greens and arugula. Tahini was swapped out for sunflower seed butter and green tea for chamomile. Luckily, avocados still were on the approved list. The results from these dietary changes on my digestion were immediate.

Beth also suggested taking two new tests: Genova GI effects, a comprehensive stool test and Genova Triad, a blood spot profile. These tests would give us a better window into my digestion, nutrient deficiencies, inflammation, detoxification, and where my diet was falling short in order to continue adjusting and improving my health.

With Beth's interpretation of my genetic testing and blood work, I was getting closer to achieving Super Balance – the state in which all of the body's systems function harmoniously and optimal health is achieved. Maintaining that balance, however, was an ongoing challenge. Regarding the many demands of business, family, friends, travel, and entertainment, I always asked myself: Is this good for my body? How will doing X or eating Y or doing Z make me feel?

- Should I meet the girls to walk in the park if I've been out late the previous night? NO
- Is it better to sleep another hour? YES
- Should I have breakfast before leaving for the airport? YES
- Is it better to prepare my healthy foods at home or go out to a restaurant? STAY HOME

Asking these questions, in conjunction with genetic testing, proper nutrition, exercise, sleep, and stress reduction is what led to better overall health. These practices need to be incorporated into our health system. If everyone would get on board with this approach to wellness, the vast majority of illnesses would be prevented. We would save the country billions of dollars in healthcare costs, and everyone would be on the path to achieve SuperBalance.

Chapter Twelve
Spring 2016

April

Pure Liquid B12 Extract

After the Triad and GI analysis test results came back, Beth informed me that my body was not methylating B12 effectively. She suggested that I stop the methyl CpG and take pure liquid B12 sublingually. It was a surprise to me that my body was not absorbing B12 as my regular blood tests indicated very high levels. Beth assured me that I would feel much better when the B12 was absorbed into my body on a cellular level. So, out with the Methyl CpG and in with the pure B12 extract drops!

How could anyone have a clue what they were absorbing or not without doing these tests to evaluate? Our genetics and personal biochemistry are unique and need to be treated accordingly through individualized testing, which to my complete bewilderment, is not available in the state of New York.

After a couple of days taking the B12, my energy increased dramatically. I had more endurance to walk in the park and around town, which meant I could do more in a day. The introduction of liquid B12 was instrumental in moving my energy, health, and stamina forward.

May

My Wellness Partner

One night in May, for the first time in almost three years, I was able to go out wearing two-inch heels. The occasion was a black tie event at the Mandarin Oriental Hotel for Solving Kids Cancer. Among the many honorees was a girl named Daniella and her parents, Lindy and Thomas, my dear friends. This was an inspiring evening of hope and survival. The night was capped off with Rachel Platten's "Fight Song," in honor of Cali, an ovarian cancer survivor, who was diagnosed at the age of 15. The lyrics are a rally cry for the power of positive thinking:

> This is my fight song
> Take back my life song
> Prove I'm alright song
> My power's turned on
> Starting right now I'll be strong
> I'll play my fight song
> And I don't really care if nobody else believes
> 'Cause I've still got a lot of fight left in me

There was not a dry eye in the room.

Later in the month at the next consultation, Beth and I discussed the state of my health to assess where I was and where it could improve further. I was very interested in how my genetics affected my metabolism. As much of the conversation and some of the terminology were beyond my comprehension, I asked her to send me an email about what we discussed. I've included her email here in its entirety to communicate and emphasize both the complexity and the importance of our work together.

May 24, 2016

Hi Linda,

It was good speaking with you today! I am so glad that you are feeling better and better each time we speak.

The next step is to support the inflammation that you have with vitamin E as well as vitamin C. This is going to help lower the oxidation that we see to the DNA on the marker #29 on the Triad test, which is elevated when there is oxidation to the guanine base of the DNA. Inflammation is a normal part of our metabolism and increasing your antioxidant status will help to squelch and lower this marker.

We discussed a lot today about MTHFR and the methylation hub of enzymes and how they affect our nutritional biochemistry. You specifically asked me to write my explanation on "polymorphisms" to our DNA and what that meant, so here it is:

Our DNA is the blueprint for the recreation of the proteins in our body. The enzymes in our body propel the biochemical reactions forward and set the environment so the chemical reactions can occur at a faster rate. Since the enzymes are made of proteins and proteins are from the DNA, we inherit our unique biochemistry from our parents. When there is a change in what is expected in a protein sequence, it is called "polymorphism" and this change will usually slow down the effectiveness of the enzyme. If there is heterozygous polymorphism with an enzyme it usually just shows the functionality of the enzyme by about 30% and it doesn't usually produce noticeable symptoms, so it can go without being addressed.

But if there is a homozygous polymorphism – which means that there is a change in the structure of the protein inherited by both parents – then this can slow the enzyme down by about 70%, which is significant especially if it's a major enzyme complex. Most enzymes require cofactors in the form of vitamins or minerals and so there is a slowing down because of genetics and also missing co-factors, which can lead to more unwanted symptoms.

If you have any more questions about anything we discussed today, please let me know! We are sending you the supplements:

- Liquid B12 ND
- Flora Myces
- Digestzymes
- Ultra Gamma E
- Stella C
- CatecholaCalm
- Folate (400mcg)

It was a pleasure speaking with you. Hope that you have a great month and enjoy your traveling. Happy summer!

Thank you,
Beth

It is wonderful to work with Beth and have her examine my genes, recommend various tests, and interpret them for me. As biologically unique individuals, it is so important to have a partner in health. What a fascinating journey to health and wellness.

June 1, 2016

Getting My Life Back After Three Years

This day marks exactly three years since I experienced my first symptoms of tingling in my hands. One day I was in Memphis, TN, at Carolyn's surprise birthday celebration and twelve days later, I was admitted to the emergency unit for treatment of Guillain-Barré syndrome. Three years later, I woke up and met Didi, Carolyn, and Lyanne to walk in the park from 8 – 9:30 am]. It was a glorious morning with clear blue skies and a cool breeze. It was a miracle that I was able to walk at all.

I've gone through so much and feel very lucky to be well and strong again. Some of my success is due to an ongoing desire to learn more about my body. Understanding my metabolism and the way my body functions has been a challenge. Guided by Beth, I have been able to restore my health and achieve SuperBalance. The genetic testing, stool analysis, Triad blood tests, a keen discipline to follow a micro nutritious diet, and reduce my toxic load have contributed to the positive results I've been fortunate enough to have achieved.

One day while playing with my granddaughters in my apartment, Alessandra (age 6 at the time) looked up at me and said, "Lili, you are very old and wise with sparkling eyes and I want you to live to 100!" What a beautiful wish.

This season, I've been able to make plans to go to the Basel Art Fair, Zurich, and London for business. My schedule is packed and I'm confident that I will manage it all very well. My anxiety, discomfort, and fear are gone. My life is open before me and I could not possibly be more grateful.

Conclusion

Functional Medicine Is the Answer

My ultimate goal for sharing my story is to inspire people to find their unique path to wellness and to take control of their health in order to find SuperBalance with diet and lifestyle changes.

Once the mystery of health was revealed to me – after three years of anxiety, fear, discomfort, and an aggressive pharmaceutical regimen – I was able to identify the weak links in my body. Through genetic and cellular blood tests, eating the correct foods, and taking the appropriate supplements for my unique self, I learned how to get well and stay well. When it all came together, the solution seemed simple, although it took a long time to find it. The path to wellness required a lot of guidance, which came from fifteen different doctors and practitioners and countless hours of independent research using resources available online.

One of the key things I learned throughout my autoimmune ordeal is that everybody is different. There is no such thing as a one-size-fits-all approach to health. There is no magic pill, shot, drip, or surgery to rid the body of inflammation and disease. If your best friend doesn't eat dairy, salt, or fat, it doesn't mean that is the right solution for you. Just because someone else had success with steroids or chemotherapy, doesn't mean that you will too.

We all metabolize foods, supplements, and pharmaceuticals differently according to our unique DNA. Discovering what I needed to fuel and balance my individual biochemistry was what ultimately led to my renewed energy, strength, and vitality.

Given all that I have learned and been through, I developed a strong desire to help others to make the connection between healthy eating for their individual DNA and the resulting improvements in their overall health. Once the systems in the body are functioning properly, there are many amazing results including extra weight comes off; blood pressure and sugar normalize. People who are diagnosed with an autoimmune disorder are prone to cascading issues if the root cause is not resolved, which is why working with a nutritionist trained in Functional Medicine is of the utmost importance.

The following routine is what works for me. Find out what works for you and seek your own SuperBalance.

1. Sleep: 7 – 9 hours; essential for detoxification and regeneration of the body.

2. Food: a diet rich in omega 3s and essential fatty acids. No gluten, no dairy, and very little sugar (but I can't live without my gluten-free dark chocolate every day).

3. Personalized supplements: digestive enzymes, folate, B12, biotin, Vitamins C, D, and E, glutamine powder, and floramyces probiotics.

4. Exercise: Daily morning walks in Central Park at 8 am, daily yoga stretches, weights 3x week, and balance exercises on the bosu ball.

5. Water: 6 – 8 glasses of filtered water daily or 50% of your body weight

6. Manage stress: Worrying raises cortisol levels and solves nothing. The burden is on each one of us to look at our lives and remove as much stress as possible. Eliminate the things you cannot control or change (i.e.: breaking news) and focus on the things you can control (i.e.: what you consume and your lifestyle).

7. Always be positive: This means having a Plan B and going all the way to Z if necessary.

Let's all work together toward a new future of healthcare; one in which patients are empowered to ask questions and participate, and doctors are trained to look at patients as a whole person to devise individual protocols. When a patient is sick, the doctor explains there is a way to reverse illness and there is hope to get well! Thus, a partnership between doctors and patients is formed.

The initial appointment takes about two hours, during which time the doctor gets to know the patient and their lifestyle, eating/sleeping habits, stress level, medical history, and emotional well being. The patient takes responsibility for her or his health, adopts a mindset of wellness, and becomes an active participant in getting better.

Put the billions of dollars that go into research for new drugs for disease treatment into the land. Bring nutritious and healthy food to all food markets, school cafeterias, airports, offices, and factories. The appropriate healthy food is the medicine that fuels and repairs the body and prevents disease. The focus for healthcare must be on nutrition and what functions different foods perform to diversify the gut bacteria and keep the internal systems working together.

We need a new model for a population that suffers from more chronic illnesses than ever in our history. The microbiome should be the key area of focus. There is plenty of money to be made by shifting research into this expanding field. I can see it now: Microbiome tests for $19.95 on Amazon.com. The way to health is through the gut! It's not that hard to imagine; the future of my dreams is within our grasp.

In a recent podcast, James Maskell, Founder of the Evolution of Medicine and Host of the Functional Forum, quotes R. Buckminster Fuller: "You never change things by fighting the existing reality. To change something, build a new model that makes the existing model obsolete."

What's Next?

My New Project, SuperBalance™

In 2022, almost nine years after my diagnosis and six years after I regained my health, I am introducing my new platform, SuperBalance™! Though it is based on my personal experience, it will expand to support anyone who wants to improve their health.

SuperBalance™ will focus on creating a community of wellness, guidance and empowerment for people to take their health into their own hands. SuperBalance™ recently launched its website and my team and I look forward to welcoming you to the Functional Medicine Community!

You can visit the SuperBalance™ website at superbalancellc.com

References

Agus, Dr. David B., *The End of Illness* , 2012

Bland, Dr. Jeffrey S., *The Disease Delusion, Conquering the Causes of Chronic Illness for a Healthier, Longer, and Happier Life*, 2014

Blaser, Dr. Martin J., *Missing Microbes: How the Overuse of Antibiotics is Fueling our Modern Plagues*, 2014

Breuss, Michael Dr., *The Power of When: Discover Your Chronotype and the Best Time to Eat Lunch, Ask for a Raise, Have Sex, Write a Novel, Take Your Meds and More*, 2016

Brogan, Dr. Kelly, *A Mind of Your Own: The Truth About Depression and How women Can Heal Their Bodies and Reclaim Their Lives*, 2016

Chatterjee, Dr. Rangan, *How To Make Disease Disappear*, 2018

Cole, Dr. Will, *The Inflammation Spectrum*, 2019

Coles, Dr. L. Stephen, *Extraordinary Healing*, 2011

Enders, Giulia, *Gut: The Inside Story of Our Body's Most Under-Rated Organ*, 2014

Fasano, Dr. Alessio, *Gluten Freedom*, 2014

Fitzgerald, Dr. Kara , *Younger You*, 2020

Fletcher, Emily, *Stress Less, Accomplish MORE, Meditation for Extraordinary Performance*, 2019

Fogg, BJ, PhD, TINY HABITS, *The Small Changes that Change Everything*, 2020

Francis, Raymond, *The Great American Health Hoax: The Surprising Truth About How Modern Medicine Makes You Sick*, 2015

Galland, Dr. Leo, *Power Healing*, 1998

Gonzalez, Dr. Nicholas J., *Nutrition and the Autonomic Nervous System*, 2017

Gordon, Dr. James S., *Manifesto For A New Medicine, Your Guide to Healing Partnerships and the Wise Use of Alternative Therapies*, 1996

Junger, Dr. Alejandro, *Clean, Remove, Restore, Rejuvenate*, 2009

Hawkins, Dr. David R., *Letting Go: The Pathway of Surrender*, 2012

Hyman, Dr. Mark, *The Blood Sugar Solution: 10- Day Detox Diet*, 2014

Hyman, Dr. Mark, *Eat Fat, Get Thin: Why The Fat We Eat is Key to Sustained Weight Loss and Vibrant Health*, 2016

Hyman, Dr. Mark, FOOD *What The Heck Should I Eat?*, 2019

Hyman, Dr. Mark, FOOD FIX *How to Save Our Health, Our Economy, Our Communities, and Our Planet – One Bite at a Time*, 2020

Jensen, Sheryl, *My Grain and Brain Cookbook*, 2014

Ji, Sayer, *Regenerate, Unlocking Your Body's Radical Resilience Through The Biology*, 2020

Kahn, Dr. Imran, *The Flame Within and Autoimmune Disorders: Prevention, Risk Factors, Diagnosis and Treatments*, 2010

Kellman, Dr. Raphael, *The Microbiome Diet: The Scientifically Proven Way to Restore Your Gut Health and Achieve Permanent Weight Loss* , 2015

Latov, Dr. Norman, *Peripheral Neuropathy: When the Numbness, Weakness and Pain Won't Stop*, 2007

Elizabeth Lipski, PhD, CNS, FACN, IFMCP, *Digestive Wellness*, Strengthen the Immune System and Prevent Disease Through Healthy Digestion, 2020

Lynch, Dr. Ben, *Dirty Genes, A Breakthrough Program* TREAT THE ROOT CAUSE OF ILLNESS *and* OPTIMIZE YOUR HEALTH, 2018

Maskell, James, *The Evolution of Medicine: Join the Movement to Solve Chronic Disease and Fall Back in Love with Medicine*, 2016

Maskell, James, *The Community Cure,, Transforming Health Outcomes Together*, 2019

Meadows, Susannah, *The Other Side of Impossible: Ordinary People Who Faced Daunting Medical Challenges and Refused to Give Up*, 2017

Myers, Dr. Amy, *The Autoimmune Solution: Prevent and Reverse the Full Spectrum of Inflammatory Symptoms and Diseases*, 2015

O'Bryan, Dr. Tom, *The Autoimmune Fix: How To Stop The Hidden Autoimmune Damage*, 2016

Ornish, Dr. Dean and Anne Ornish, *UnDo It!, How Simple Lifestyle Changes Can Reverse Most Chronic Diseases*, 2019

Osborne, Dr. Peter, *No Grain, No Pain: A 30-Day Diet for Eliminating the Root Cause of Chronic Pain*, 2016

Pedre, Dr. Vincent, *Happy Gut: The Cleansing Program to Help You Lose Weight, Gain Energy and Eliminate Pain*, 2015

Perlmutter, Dr. David, Brain Maker: *The Power of the Gut Microbes to Heal and Protect Your Brain*, 2015

Perlmutter, Dr. David, Grain Brain: *The Surprising Truth about Wheat, Carbs, and Sugar, Your Brain's Silent Killers*, 2013

Pineault, Nicolas, *The Non-Tinfoil Guide to EMFS*, 2017

Pitchford, Paul, *Healing with Whole Foods: Asian Traditions and Modern Nutrition*, 1993

Pizzorno, Dr. Joseph, *The Toxic Solution: How Hidden Poisons in the Air, Water, Food and Products We Use Are Destroying Our Health—And What We Can Do to Fix It*, 2017

Rankin, Dr. Lissa, *Mind Over Medicine: Scientific Proof That You Can Heal Yourself*, 2011

Rau, Dr. Thomas, *The Swiss Secret for Optimal Health*, 2009

Shoenfeld, Dr. Yehuda, *Mosaic of Autoimmunity, The Novel Factors of Autoimmune Disease*, 2019

Somers, Suzanne, *From Toxic to Not Sick*, 2016

Vargo, John, *Green Intelligence: Creating Environments that Protect Human Health*, Yale University Press, 2009

Wahls, Dr. Terry, *The Wahls Protocol: How I Beat Progressive MS Using Paleo Principles and Functional Medicine*, 2014

Yong, Ed, *I Contain Multitudes: The Microbes Within Us and a Grander View of Life*, 2016

About the Author

Linda R. Silverman is the CEO and founder of SuperBalanceLLC, a platform to educate people who have autoimmune disorders. Her mission is to inspire people to be part of the paradigm shift in our healthcare system. As she became knowledgeable about the cutting edge information and followed her unique path to wellness with the guidance of her nutritionist, she achieved vibrant health after several months. She continues to live the SuperBalance Lifestyle every day. She is a well established art advisor and a former director of the Contemporary Art Department at Sotheby's, New York.

superbalancellc.com

info@superbalance.org

@superbalancellc on Instagram

Made in the USA
Middletown, DE
14 October 2023